At Issue

Corporate Corruption

W9-CON-304

Other Books in the At Issue Series:

At Issue

Corporate Corruption

Judeen Bartos, Book Editor

GREENHAVEN PRESS
A part of Gale, Cengage Learning

GALE
CENGAGE Learning™

Detroit • New York • San Francisco • New Haven, Conn • Waterville, Maine • London

Elizabeth Des Chenes, *Managing Editor*

© 2012 Greenhaven Press, a part of Gale, Cengage Learning.

Gale and Greenhaven Press are registered trademarks used herein under license.

For more information, contact:
Greenhaven Press
27500 Drake Rd.
Farmington Hills, MI 48331-3535
Or you can visit our Internet site at gale.cengage.com

For product information and technology assistance, contact us at

Gale Customer Support, 1-800-877-4253
For permission to use material from this text or product, submit all requests online at
www.cengage.com/permissions

Further permissions questions can be e-mailed to permissionrequest@cengage.com

Articles in Greenhaven Press anthologies are often edited for length to meet page requirements. In addition, original titles of these works are changed to clearly present the main thesis and to explicitly indicate the author's opinion. Every effort is made to ensure that Greenhaven Press accurately reflects the original intent of the authors. Every effort has been made to trace the owners of copyrighted material.

Cover image copyright Illustration Works.

LIBRARY OF CONGRESS CATALOGING-IN-PUBLICATION DATA

Corporate corruption / Judeen Bartos, book editor.
   p. cm. -- (At issue)
Includes bibliographical references and index.
   ISBN 978-0-7377-5560-2 (hardcover) -- ISBN 978-0-7377-5561-9 (pbk.)
   1. Corporations--Corrupt practices. 2. Business ethics. 3. Corporate governance.
I. Bartos, Judeen.
   HF5387.C66792 2011
   174'.4--dc22
                                           2011014468

Printed in the United States of America
1 2 3 4 5   15 14 13 12 11

ED230

Contents

Introduction

Corruption and greed among America's corporate entities has resulted in a reduction in public trust and confidence vital to a healthy society. Each act of deception or betrayal has contributed to the economic troubles facing our world today in ways both direct and indirect. The more sensational examples of wrongdoing such as the scandals involving investment broker Bernie Madoff, and companies such as Enron and Halliburton have entered the language as shorthand for corrupt behavior. The public clamors for more laws and regulations, while an equally large outcry erupts from businesses claiming that overly strict regulation makes it harder for America to compete globally.

Many observers note that profit has become the sole driving force in many corporations, who ignore the impact their actions have on the economy, society, or the environment. The conduct of some major health insurance providers serves as an example. Health insurance companies have dropped seriously ill policyholders so they can meet "Wall Street's relentless profit expectations", testified former Cigna senior executive Wendell Potter during a Senate hearing on health insurance in June 2009. While the devastating outcome of this practice for the individual policyholder is readily apparent, the repercussions can affect many more.

The *American Journal of Medicine* published the results of a national study in 2009 indicating that "medical reasons" was the number one cause of bankruptcy filings by individuals in 2007. Sixty-two percent of these filings were a result of medical debt or loss of income due to serious illness. Surprisingly, the study noted that three quarters of the individuals who filed for bankruptcy as a result of medical debt had health insurance. Bankruptcies filed due to medical debt can also result in the loss of an individual's home and a significant lowering in the economic status of entire families. Neighborhoods can be negatively impacted by the presence of a foreclosed home by causing a decrease in surrounding property values. Individuals may need to obtain governmental assistance such as Medicare or Social Security disability, increasing the financial responsibility of society as a whole for their care and support.

The impact of bankruptcies as a result of medical debt or lack of good medical insurance are but one illustration of the far-reaching consequences of corporate corruption driven by greed and profit. The deceptive behavior of a health insurance company, who looks for ways to drop its sick policyholders, provides a profit for a few at the expense of many. As corporations grow increasingly wealthy and more powerful, American citizens have less ability to regulate and restrict the actions of large companies. Democracy in America faces a serious threat as corporations wield their money and influence on the political process in order to coerce politicians to enact laws favorable to their bottom lines.

Although breaking this seemingly endless cycle seems daunting, there are voices calling for a new business model that takes a more inclusive, long-term view. Michael E. Porter and Mark R. Kramer are two observers who argue that America's current approach is an outdated one. In their February 2011 article in the *Harvard Business Review* titled, "The Big Idea: Creating Shared Value", Porter and Kramer state that companies "continue to view value creation narrowly, optimizing short-term financial performance in a bubble while missing the most important customer needs and ignoring the broader influences that determine their long-term success."

Porter and Kramer believe that "businesses must reconnect company success with social progress." They put forth a solution they call *Shared Value*, "which involves creating economic value in a way that *also* creates value for society by addressing its needs and challenges." They point out that a number of companies are embracing the concept of shared value, and implementing practices that show a greater appreciation for their role in society. Industry leaders such as General Electric (GE), Google, and WalMart have set out to redefine their purpose in a way that is not solely focused on short-term profits.

There is also a growing chorus challenging the rationale that American companies need to be profit-focused in order to compete with emerging economic powers such as China and India. They dispute the notion that in order to stay competitive in the global market, America needs to copy the practices of developing economies. Emerging industrial nations like China and India have low production and labor costs, resulting in lower priced goods. Critics argue that American industries decrease wages and benefits of their own workers in an attempt to mimic these other countries, and that these practices have done far more harm than good.

Sam Pizzigati, a labor journalist for the online newsletter, *Too Much*, asserts in his February 2011 column that Scandinavian nations, including Norway, Sweden, Finland, and Denmark, provide a better example of how to remain competitive in a global market. The four nations presented a report called "The Nordic Way" at the World Economic Forum in January 2011 that outlined the ways in which they retain a distinct competitive edge. As a result, the Nordics have survived the ongoing recession with much healthier economies than most other developed nations, Pizzigati reports.

The Nordic nations provide their citizens a "strong social safety net," noted Norway's prime minister Jens Stoltenberg at the Davos World Economic Forum in 2011, while making sure that businesses have "low transaction costs," in part because businesses operating in these countries are not hampered by expensive paperwork and legalities. By making investment in their human capital a priority, these nations, according to Pizzigati, cultivate a socially cohesive society that nurtures a high degree of trust between the private and public sector. This spirit of cooperation reflects a value they hold highly, said Stoltenberg: "there is no contradiction between social equality and economic efficiency."

If companies remain dedicated to a mindset that pursues profits at all costs, corruption will never be far behind. There will always be the temptation to find a way, legal or not, to maximize wealth. But if enough companies come to the realization that this is not sustainable as a business model or as a society, there is a real chance that corporate corruption will become a rarity. Further, companies will discover they can succeed within a framework that benefits everyone.

1

Secret Campaign Funding Corrupts and Endangers Democracy

David Corn

David Corn is a political journalist and author, and serves as the Washington bureau chief for Mother Jones. *He has appeared regularly on Fox News, MSNBC, and National Public Radio.*

Critics of the Supreme Court's Citizens United *ruling feared the new law would adversely affect the 2010 elections and it appears they may have been correct. An unprecedented amount of money was spent on this election, much of it anonymously, since campaign finance reform was put into place following the aftermath of the Watergate scandal in the mid-1970s.*

Advocates have tried to limit the influence of special interest groups on American elections for many years, but the system makes it easy for special interest groups to virtually buy politicians, who depend on financing provided by these groups in order to stay in office. The anonymity of this type of political funding is especially troubling as a small number of wealthy individuals are behind much of the spending and can strongly impact the political landscape for their own personal or corporate gain in a way that ordinary voters cannot.

One result of the 2010 campaign is clear before any ballots are counted: Democracy is in danger.

That sounds hyperbolic. But whatever remains of the quaint notion—call it a myth—that in a democracy citizens

David Corn, "And 2010's Biggest Winner Is . . ." *Mother Jones*, November 2, 2010. © Copyright 2010 Foundation for National Progress. All rights reserved. Reproduced by permission.

are more or less equal is in the process of being shredded, due to the rise this year of super PACs [Political Action Committee] and secretive political nonprofits. Thanks to the Supreme Court's notorious *Citizens United* decision and other rulings, a small number of well-heeled individuals (or corporations or unions) can now amass a tremendous amount of political influence by throwing an unlimited amount of money into efforts to elect their preferred candidates. And certain political nonprofits, such as Crossroads GPS—the outfit set up this year by GOP [Grand Old Party, or Republican] strategists Karl Rove and Ed Gillespie (which with an affiliated group is spending about $50 million)—can pour tens of millions of dollars into the elections without revealing the source of their campaign cash.

Unprecedented Spending

The secret and unlimited flow of dollars into congressional campaigns this year is largely unprecedented—at least since campaign finance reform was implemented following Watergate in the 1970s. Almost half a trillion dollars have been spent so far by outside groups—with about one-quarter of that coming from dark-money groups that don't disclose donors. And it's not just a Republican phenomenon. Unions and Democratic-leaning advocacy outfits are playing the game. Still, the advantage goes to the GOP. Of the outside groups not connected to either political party, those supporting Republicans and opposing Democrats have so far spent $119.2 million, and those supporting Democrats and opposing Republicans have dumped $73.8 million into races. This split is dramatic, but there's another factor to consider: Much of the pro-Democratic money comes from large membership groups (including the SEIU [Service Employees International Union] and the National Education Association), yet much of the pro-Republican money originates from a small number of millionaires (or billionaires). Consequently, fat cats have gained even more disproportionate influence.

The White House has complained about the rise of super PACs and the spread of secret money, though it miscalculated by focusing on the possible flow of foreign money into these endeavors—blasting the Chamber of Commerce's pro-Republican efforts—when the issue is the overall boost in special interest money. And here's the kicker: The 2010 campaign is merely a warmup for 2012 and campaigns after that.

Local television station owners, your payday has come. Secret money will flow before, during, and after elections.

Corporate Money Is Calling the Shots Year-Round

It doesn't take a *New York Times* article—such as the one headlined "Conservative Donor Groups Lay a Base for 2012 Elections"—to predict what's coming. The permanent, never-ending campaign will become even more permanent and nev-erending. These big-and-secret-money groups will be working 24/7, opposing and discrediting President Barack Obama and the Democrats in the so-called off-year and then revving up for the 2012 presidential and congressional elections. The negative ads never have to stop. ("President Obama and Rep-resentative [fill in the name of a local House Democrat] are trying to ruin this nation's future with their reckless and risky schemes to [expand government spending/raise taxes/provide amnesty to illegal immigrants/Impose socialized medicine on American families].") Surely, Rove and others can find enough right-wing millionaires to underwrite a constant blitzkrieg against Obama and the Democrats.

The argument for this is an obvious one: It will soften up the Dems for the final kill in 2012. Rep. Tom Perriello, the in-cumbent House Democrat freshman in Virginia's 5th Con-gressional District, has faced such a daunting reelection this year partly because outside conservative and corporate groups started running ads against him soon after he took office in January 2009. Perriello stood out as a target, given that he won by a measly 727 votes in a GOP-friendly district. But if enough money is bagged, Rove and his comrades will be able to target not just out-on-a-limb Democrats but a host of House and Senate Democrats year-round. Local television station owners, your payday has come. Secret money will flow before, during, and after elections.

Campaign finance reform advocates are in total despair. For decades, they have tried to lessen the impact of special interest money on the political system. (The House Democrats passed Obama-backed legislation earlier this year to force disclosure of contributors, but the bill stalled in the GOP-obstructed Senate.) Now the dam seems gone, blown up, in rubble. Moreover, the Federal Election Commission, which is responsible for enforcing the campaign finance rules that still exist, is in shambles. And the Internal Revenue Service has not yet demonstrated an ability or willingness to go after the political nonprofits under its jurisdiction, which may be violating IRS (Internal Revenue Service) rules that supposedly limit their campaign-related activities. (And how bad would it be for any of these groups to be slapped with an IRS fine after succeeding in changing the political landscape?)

Democrats Are in a Bind

All this places Obama in a jam. Does he continue to decry the rise of super PACs and secret-donor nonprofits? Or does he encourage Democrats to fight big-secret money with big-secret money of their own? In the past, the Democrats have had success marshaling such resources. . . . But can Obama do both—assail the new campaign finance order and explain that Democrats have no choice but to play by these anti-democratic rules? Mixed messages tend not to resonate well with voters. If Obama signals Democrats that he'd like them to unleash their own big-money hounds, he will likely find it tough to score political points by opposing the GOP's big-money efforts. Then again, can racking up debate points help Obama and his Democrats stand up to a tsunami of campaign cash? It's a dilemma.

The election news ... will naturally focus on who won and who lost and the subsequent shift in the balance of power in Washington. But this campaign season has brought about a profound and fundamental shift in systemic, money-based political power. And it's far from done.

2

The Rights of Corporations Should Not Trump the Rights of Individuals

Rand Clifford

Rand Clifford is a novelist and essayist living in Spokane, Washington.

The American people are experiencing a reduced role in the democratic process. While the January 2010 Citizens United Supreme Court decision, which removed important restrictions on the amount of money corporations can spend in elections, will no doubt have a tremendous impact on future election results, another ruling by the high court is actually responsible for giving corporations the same rights as US citizens. A May 26, 1886 decision made corporations "artificial persons", entitled to all the same rights and protections of human citizens.

This decision made little sense then and has proven damaging to average American lives ever since, allowing corporations to grow ever more powerful until little can be done to protect the 'common good' versus the pursuit of profit that seems to be the primary goal of almost every corporation.

Ray Davies, front man for the British rock band The Kinks, sang in 1974: "*I can visualize the day when the world will be controlled by artificial people, but I don't want to live a lie in an artificial world.*"

Rand Clifford, "Artificial People: End Corporate Personhood. Corporations are Not People" GlobalResearch.ca, September 14, 2010. Copyright © 2010 by GlobalResearch.ca. Reproduced by permission.

The song is titled, "Artificial Man," from the album, *Preservation Act II*. Ray Davies' words were very apropos in 1974, even more so in 2010—especially with the fresh Supreme Court of the United States (SCOTUS) ruling that dissolves any restrictions on the amount of money corporations may spend to influence elections. By overruling two important precedents regarding the 1st amendment rights of corporations, the SCOTUS opened the floodgates, allowing unlimited corporate cash to inundate elections, thereby further depleting the already meager power of actual American people to choose our elected officials and influence America's future course.

Yes, the first elections to be flooded with unlimited corporate cash will be this November, and polls are clearly showing a profound influence. The "grand old party" that usurped the wheel of power in 2000 inherited a balanced budget, then drove the nation off the road, into a very deep ditch of debt and slime. They oversaw unprecedented upward transfer of wealth, lied us into unwinnable wars for oil, pipeline routes, and heroin, leaving over a million dead and millions more homeless. They poured gasoline on the flames of global hatred toward America, ravaged our middle class and labor unions while stripping rights out of our Constitution in the name of "homeland security". They grinned at corporate bottom lines as millions of American jobs were "off-shored" to capitalize on foreign slave labor. And don't forget 9/11—not the official whitewash fantasies, but what actually happened what virtually all of the evidence says, evidence which was not destroyed as quickly as possible. The overtly illegitimate and criminal [George W.] Bush II administration and their neocons [neo-conservatives] were not simply ". . . asleep at the wheel" on 9/11, they pulled off stellar false flag terror, considering all of the damage wrought, including the farcical war on terror, another mechanism of pushing more wealth up to the wealthy.

In the most important ways for the common good, it was the darkest eight years in American "history". And now, Social Security is already being called an "entitlement", as though recipients haven't paid into it all their working lives. If you want to see total chaos, wait until the GOP [Grand Old Party; the Republican Party] kills Social Security. . . .

Candidates with the most campaign cash usually win, especially those with gobs of cash.

Flood of Corporate Money Influences Elections

After miring us so deeply in the ditch, then spending two years licking their wounds and obstructing almost any attempts to get us back on the road, Republicans are having mass Pavlovian responses regarding their prospects in November—thanks to corporations flooding them with election cash same as BPs [British Petroleum] Macondo well flooded the Gulf of Mexico with oil. And remember, the Macondo well is not yet safely sealed . . . may never be safely sealed. Seen any CorpoMedia *news* about what is going on under the Macondo wellhead lately? Damage down below is apparently so extensive that BP is afraid to do anything about a permanent seal, while the government . . . well, in certain financial ways, BP is the government. . . .

Our dilemma is simple. Candidates with the most campaign cash usually win, especially those with gobs of cash. Under the new rules, corporations can control elections to such a degree as to make them a bad joke. So, our electorate becomes corporate stooges top to bottom, and corporate cash is magnetized to flow to the right. Hard right.

Our solution is also simple, yet daunting. End corporate personhood. Somehow get the SCOTUS to rule that corporations are not people, and should not enjoy the same rights as

"All persons born or naturalized in the United States and of the State wherein they reside" (from the 14th amendment). So how did corporations become people? Illegally . . . not to mention nonsensically.

The core problem stems from an 1886 SCOTUS ruling that was not actually a ruling—but that hasn't stopped it from being perhaps the most malign thing the SCOTUS has ever done regarding the common good of America . . . perhaps the most damaging precedent the common good has ever paid for.

The History of Corporate Personhood

We might consider May 26, 1886, to be the *birthday* of official American corporate personhood. Court reporter J.C. Bancroft Davis wrote a letter to Chief Justice Morrison R. Waite, in essence asking to include in the headnotes informal conversation implying that all justices agreed, in the Santa Clara County versus Southern Pacific Railroad case, that the 14th amendment to the Constitution applies to corporations. Waite answered somewhat cryptically that Davis should make the decision as to headnotes of the case.

So how did corporations become people? Illegally . . . not to mention nonsensically.

The 14th amendment was originally established to protect and preserve the lives, property and freedoms of Americans from repressive government. Suddenly, corporations were people, gaining the legal status of citizens—again, not by a new Supreme Court interpretation of the fourteenth amendment, as commonly thought, but by a former railroad company president acting as court reporter maneuvering the "ruling" into the books. Instant landmark *ruling*! Corporations became "artificial persons" with rights of a citizen, plus many advantages such as immortality, mega cash flow, the ability to be many places at once, etc.. Soon after, John D. Rockefeller, father of the modern corporation, created the Standard Oil Corporation. And by the late 1880s, over 90% of American oil refineries were controlled by Standard Oil.

Do you know any person who does not breathe, eat, drink, sleep, bleed when you prick them, or was not born either male or female? Yes, you do, they are called corporations, and we are racing toward a world controlled by corporations. Most people believe, at least those not masters of most of America's wealth, that the nation is careening drastically off course. Heaping more power onto the most corporate of our two leading political parties, the one that mired us so deeply in the ditch last time they were in power, seems a tidy fit with the definition of insanity. Things are so bad there are even growing cries for revolution, and secession—even a burgeoning new party secretly financed by corporations *themselves*.

Perhaps one of the most beneficial changes for the common good, one that may even inject the withered notion of "common good" itself into our corporate-dominated political landscape, would be for enough actual people to come to their senses to empower a real grassroots movement focused on reversing the legal status of corporations as people, which they are so obviously not. As stacked against real people (to a thoughtful person, is there really any other kind?) as the odds are, there still might be some chance. What chance will there be when over 90% of America will be ". . . controlled by artificial people," and the GOP is restored to full power?

The last line of Ray Davies' song, "Artificial Man":

"We went and built a master race, to live within our artificial world."

3

Corporations Can Behave Ethically and Thrive

The Economist

The Economist is a weekly news publication based in London.

There is a commonly held belief among many corporations that the only way to succeed in business is to engage in unethical behavior. But a growing body of evidence suggests otherwise. Numerous large corporations, such as IKEA, Reebok, and Google have prospered without resorting to bribery and corrupt practices. In fact, the price of engaging in corruption has been shown to actually have a counter-productive effect.

America and Britain are leading a worldwide effort to combat corruption by putting legislative and monetary teeth into pursuing companies that break the law. Cooperation among nations means that corporations are increasingly unable to move their operations to countries who ignore business and ethical violations. The result has been a marked increase in the number of cross-border investigations and prosecutions. Corporations would be best served to forgo the short term benefits that corruption may bring and focus on building a reputable business that will prosper in the long run.

It is 15 years since Moisés Naím coined the memorable phrase "corruption eruption". But there is no sign of the eruption dying down. Indeed, there is so much molten lava and sulphurous ash around that some of the world's biggest companies have been covered in it. Siemens and Daimler have

The Economist, "The Corruption Eruption," April 29, 2010. Copyright © 2010 by The Economist Newspaper Group (New York). Reproduced by permission.

recently been forced to pay gargantuan fines. BHP Billiton, a giant mining company, has admitted that it may have been involved in bribery. America's Department of Justice is investigating some 150 companies, targeting oil and drugs firms in particular.

The ethical case against corruption is too obvious to need spelling out. But many companies still believe that, in this respect at least, there is a regrettable tension between the dictates of ethics and the logic of business. Bribery is the price that you must pay to enter some of the world's most difficult markets (the "when in Rome" argument). Bribery can also speed up the otherwise glacial pace of bureaucracy (the "efficient grease" hypothesis). And why not? The chances of being caught are small while the rewards for bending the rules can be big and immediate.

The hidden costs of corruption are almost always much higher than companies imagine.

Bribery Is Not Necessary nor Effective in the Long Run

But do you really have to behave like a Roman to thrive in Rome? Philip Nichols, of the Wharton School, points out that plenty of Western firms have prospered in emerging markets without getting their hands dirty, including Reebok, Google and Novo Nordisk. IKEA has gone to great lengths to fight corruption in Russia, including threatening to halt its expansion in the country, firing managers who pay bribes and buying generators to get around grasping officials holding up grid connections. What is more, Mr Nichols argues, it is misguided to dismiss entire countries as corrupt. Even the greasiest-palmed places are in fact ambivalent about corruption: they invariably have laws against it and frequently produce politicians who campaign against it. Multinationals should help bolster the rules of the game rather than pandering to the most unscrupulous players.

And is "grease" really all that efficient? In a paper published by the World Bank, Daniel Kaufmann and Shang-Jin Wei subjected the "efficient grease" hypothesis to careful scrutiny. They found that companies that pay bribes actually end up spending more time negotiating with bureaucrats. The prospect of a pay-off gives officials an incentive to haggle over regulations. The paper also found that borrowing is more expensive for corrupt companies, probably because of the regulatory flux.

The hidden costs of corruption are almost always much higher than companies imagine. Corruption inevitably begets ever more corruption: bribe-takers keep returning to the trough and bribe-givers open themselves up to blackmail. Corruption also exacts a high psychological cost on those who engage in it. Mr Nichols says that corrupt business people habitually compare their habit to having an affair: no sooner have you given in to temptation than you are trapped in a world of secrecy and guilt. On the other hand, the benefits of rectitude can be striking. Texaco, an oil giant now subsumed by Chevron, had such an incorruptible reputation that African border guards were said to wave its jeeps through without engaging in the ritual shakedown.

Moreover, the likelihood of being caught is dramatically higher than it was a few years ago. The internet has handed much more power to whistle-blowers. NGOs [nongovernmental organizations] keep a constant watch on big firms. Every year Transparency International publishes its Corruption Perceptions Index, its Bribe Payers Index and its Global Corruption Barometer.

Countries Band Together to Fight Corruption

The likelihood of prosecution is also growing. The [US President Barack] Obama administration has revamped a piece of post-Watergate legislation—the Foreign Corrupt Practices Act

(FCPA)—and is using it to pursue corporate malefactors the world over. The Department of Justice is pursuing far more cases than it ever has before: 150 today compared with just eight in 2001. And it is subjecting miscreants to much rougher treatment. Recent legislation has made senior managers personally liable for corruption on their watch. They risk a spell in prison as well as huge fines. The vagueness of the legislation means that the authorities may prosecute for lavish entertainment as well as more blatant bribes.

[T]he likelihood of being caught is dramatically higher than it was a few years ago.

America is no longer a lone ranger. Thirty-eight countries have now signed up to the OECD's [Organization for Economic Cooperation and Development] 1997 anti-corruption convention, leading to a spate of cross-border prosecutions. In February Britain's BAE Systems, a giant arms company, was fined $400m as a result of a joint British and American investigation. Since then a more ferocious Bribery Act has come into force in Britain. On April 1st [2010] Daimler was fined $185m as a result of a joint American and German investigation which examined the firm's behaviour in 22 countries.

Companies caught between these two mighty forces—the corruption and anti-corruption eruptions—need to start taking the problem seriously. A Transparency International study of 500 prominent firms revealed that the average company only scored 17 out of a possible 50 points on "anti-corruption practices" (Belgium was by far the worst performing European country). Companies need to develop explicit codes of conduct on corruption, train their staff to handle demands for pay-offs and back them up when they refuse them. Clubbing together and campaigning for reform can also help. Businesses played a leading role in Poland's Clean Hands movement, for example, and a group of upright Panamanian firms have formed an anti-corruption group.

This may all sound a bit airy-fairy given that so many companies are struggling just to survive the recession. But there is nothing airy-fairy about the $1.6 billion in fines that Siemens has paid to the American and German governments. And there is nothing airy-fairy about a spell in prison. The phrase "doing well by doing good" is one of the most irritating parts of the CSR [Corporate Social Responsibility] mantra. But when it comes to corruption, it might just fit the bill.

4

Lax Penalties Do Not Deter Corporate Wrongdoers

David Callahan

David Callahan is cofounder of Demos, a public policy institute based in New York City where he now serves as a Senior Fellow. He is author of The Cheating Culture: Why More Americans Are Doing Wrong to Get Ahead.

When it comes to white-collar crime, the punishment often does not fit the crime. In the case of Angelo Mozilo, former CEO of Countrywide Mortgage Company, the penalty consisted of a monetary fine that seemed substantial at first glance, but was minor when compared to the money Mozilo made while presiding over the company. This case is another example in a string of lightly punished crimes that ultimately do little to dissuade the next batch of criminals from wrongdoing because of the small amount of risk involved.

Let's say a business leader makes hundreds of millions of dollars through criminal practices that end up wiping out the wealth of myriad homeowners and contributing to the biggest economic crisis in 70 years. Then, as punishment, he is forced to fork over $67.5 million—and yet faces no prison time. Has justice been done?

Well, if you listen to the SEC [Securities and Exchange Commission]—and plenty of media commentators, too—the settlement just reached with former Countrywide CEO Angelo

Mozilo was tough stuff. It was reportedly among the largest fines ever imposed on an individual by the SEC. To be sure, $67.5 million is big money. Except in comparison to the fortune that Mozilo made presiding over one of the shadiest mortgage firms of all time—reportedly a half billion dollars. *Time* magazine didn't just name Mozilo one of the "25 people to blame for the financial crisis," it put him on the top of the list. Countrywide has been sued by nearly a dozen state attorney generals for its predatory lending practices. The company, now owned by Bank of America, has also been hit by a blizzard of other suits.

One reason that Mozilo got away with so much is that he effectively bribed numerous regulators and lawmakers, of both parties, with dirt cheap mortgages through his so-called "Friends of Angelo" program.

Ultimately, Mozilo wasn't even nailed for his mortgage practices. The SEC got him for insider trading and securities fraud, alleging that Mozilo unloaded Countrywide's stock on unwitting investors as the company began to tank—all the while saying that everything was fine.

An Absence of Punishment Encourages Greed

As is common in these cases, Mozilo did not acknowledge any wrongdoing as part of his settlement with the government. That outcome is reminiscent of how the corrupt financial analysts, Jack Grubman and Henry Blodget, were let off the hook. Both settled with regulators after playing key roles in the dotcom scandals of the 1990s. When those settlements were reached, many observers predicted—myself included—that the absence of any personal punishment for the analysts would encourage future greed and lawlessness.

Now the cycle is being repeated. It is hard to see how the Mozilo settlement—coming on the heels of another weak SEC settlement with financier Steve Rattner—will deter future wrongdoing. Indeed, it could have the contrary effect. If you can make a great fortune behaving badly, get busted, and still end up with most of that fortune, then you've come out way ahead. At least in financial terms.

In defense of the SEC, complex white-collar cases can be difficult to win at trial. Especially when the defendant can spend limitless amounts of money on the best legal team. And that truth, too, is well known among well-heeled criminals.

So in the end, here's the calculus that might run through the mind of an executive considering breaking the law in order to make a huge fortune: First, they probably will never get investigated. But if they do get investigated, they probably will never go to trial. But if their case does come to court, they stand a decent chance of winning by hiring superior legal firepower. And even if they lose in court, their sentence may be short and they may still end up very wealthy.

Mozilo's story is yet more testimony to the seductive power of big money in an age of soaring inequality and lax regulation.

None of this is to say that Angelo Mozilo doesn't have regrets. Like many central figures in big financial scandals, he doesn't seem like an especially bad guy. He grew up the son of a butcher and worked his way to the top of the mortgage business over many years. His intentions seemed noble at earlier points in his career, as he talked about making homes more affordable to low-income Americans. Mozilo also raised questions about Countrywide's practices. As the *New York Times* describes,

> In its complaint, the S.E.C. cited a series of e-mails written by Mr. Mozilo starting in 2006 that decried some of Countrywide's lending practices even as the company's executives publicly boasted about its high-quality loans.

"In all my years in the business, I have never seen a more toxic product," Mr. Mozilo wrote in an April 17, 2006, e-mail to Mr. Sambol [his chief financial officer], referring to loans that allowed borrowers with poor credit histories to buy homes without putting any money down.

Mr. Mozilo also warned his colleagues about the dangers of a popular type of adjustable-rate mortgage that let borrowers pay a fraction of the typical monthly charge. In an April 2006 e-mail, Mr. Mozilo wrote that he had "personally observed a serious lack of compliance within our origination system as it relates to documentation and generally a deterioration in the quality of loans originated."

And yet Mozilo let Countrywide's subprime mortgage machine march on—ultimately to disaster. Mozilo's story is yet more testimony to the seductive power of big money in an age of soaring inequality and lax regulation. It would be nice to think that this age has come to a close. But Mozilo's light punishment, with the clear message that crime pays, will help ensure that is not the case.

5

Top Executives Should Not Be Rewarded for Short-Term Results

Roland Jones

Roland Jones is a producer and senior writer/editor at msnbc .com. He joined the company from TheStreet.com where he covered Internet technology and personal finance. He previously worked as a senior editor at Thomson Financial.

Pay for chief executive officers (CEOs) is rarely tied to performance, and compensation packages have been massive for the fifty firms that have laid off the most workers since 2008. A report published by the Institute of Policy Studies analyzed the compensation practices of these firms and found the inequity to be staggering. Part of the reason lies in the structure of compensation packages given many top executives, who are rewarded in a way that encourages short-term gains. Until these practices change, executives have less incentive to pursue long-term viability strategies that are good for employees and company stockholders.

When Hewlett-Packard's [HP] Chief Executive Mark Hurd resigned last month he received something few regular workers see when they quit their jobs under a cloud: A massive payout.

Turns out Hurd is far from the only top executive to be rewarded with a rich package despite a management performance that could be considered less than optimal—especially by rank-and-file workers.

Our findings illustrate the great unfairness of the Great Recession. . . .

A new report concludes that chief executives of the 50 firms that have laid off the most workers since the onset of the economic crisis in 2008 took home 42 percent more pay in 2009 than their peers at other large U.S. companies.

The report, from the Institute of Policy Studies, found that the 50 layoff leaders received $12 million on average in 2009, compared with an average compensation of $8.5 million for chief executives of companies in Standard & Poor's 500. Each of the 50 companies examined in the report laid off at least 3,000 workers between November 2008 and April 2010.

"Our findings illustrate the great unfairness of the Great Recession," said Sarah Anderson, lead author of the study, "CEO Pay and the Great Recession," the latest in a series of annual "Executive Excess" reports published by the institute, a progressive think tank. "CEOs are squeezing workers to boost short-term profits and fatten their own paychecks."

Those CEOs include HP's Hurd, who slashed 6,400 jobs in 2009—a year when his compensation amounted to $24.2 million.

Examples of Obscene Paychecks Abound

Hurd made headlines last month when he suddenly resigned after an investigation into a sexual harassment claim against him found he had falsified expense reports related to meetings with a female contractor. Despite the findings, he walked away with a severance package that reportedly could be worth more than $40 million.

The report also highlights Johnson & Johnson's William Weldon, who took home $25.6 million—more than three times the average CEO compensation for big U.S. companies—even as the health care giant was slashing 9,000 jobs and facing a massive drug recall scandal.

Fred Hassan of drug pharmaceutical company Schering-Plough received a $33 million "golden parachute" when his firm merged with Merck in late 2009, the report said, even as Schering was laying off 16,000 workers. The report calculates that Hassan's total compensation for 2009 of almost $50 million could have been used to cover the average cost of these workers' jobless benefits for over 10 weeks.

Overall, the Institute for Policy Studies calculates that the $598 million total compensation awarded to the top 50 CEO layoff leaders was enough to provide average unemployment benefits to 37,759 workers for an entire year, or nearly one month of benefits for each of the 531,363 workers their companies laid off.

While the details of the report may seem shocking at first blush, it's worth remembering that a public company's chief executive has a fiduciary obligation to maximize value for the owners of a corporation—its shareholders.

"This report is not quite as cynical as it seems," said Dr. Andrew Ward, associate dean at the College of Business at Lehigh University in Bethlehem, Pa.

"We often find CEOs are simply taking action in the face of an economic crisis to reduce expenses," he said. "The thinking is that, in the future the company's productivity will increase (and) that it will ultimately perform more efficiently, and this usually garners a positive reaction on Wall Street."

However, one worrying aspect of the report is the finding that five of the 50 top layoff leaders received taxpayer-funded bailouts. American Express, for example, gave CEO Kenneth Chenault $16.8 million in 2009, including a $5 million cash bonus. American Express has laid off 4,000 employees since receiving $3.4 billion in taxpayer bailout funds, the report said.

"Questions should be asked of the boards of these sorts of companies," Ward said. "A company's board has a great deal of responsibility for overseeing CEO compensation."

Even among their peers, the CEOs examined in the Institute of Policy Studies report were handsomely compensated. They received average increases of 7 percent in 2009 while chief executives in Standard & Poor's 500 companies saw their pay decline around 11 percent on average, according to the institute's Anderson.

CEOs Focus on Short-Term Gains, Ignore Long-Term Costs

"What's clear here is that CEOs who slash thousands of jobs certainly aren't tightening their belts," she told CNBC in an interview. "And I would caution that while these layoffs might have boosted short-term profits in terms of cutting labor costs, such cutbacks can have long-term costs for a company in terms of lower morale and the costs associated with hiring workers down the road, so I find it a disturbing trend."

The report also highlights the structure of company pay packages and unintended consequences of tying performance to stock price, said Ward.

In the past, many companies rewarded executives with stock options, which had little downside risk and gave corporate leaders a clear incentive to drive up a company's stock price.

These days there is a movement toward rewarding corporate executives with "restricted" company stock instead that has more downside risk because it behaves like regular shares.

Employees generally may not sell restricted stock until a certain amount of time passes or a financial target has been met, and they may have to forfeit their shares if they leave a company before a certain period.

"So there's less incentive for a company executive to engage in actions in the short term that simply boost a company's stock price," Ward said. "The executive's incentives are more aligned with those of the long-term individual shareholder."

6

Wall Street Bonuses Are Important and Necessary for the Economy's Success

Roy C. Smith

Roy C. Smith is a professor of finance at New York University. He is the author of several books, including Paper Fortunes— Modern Wall Street: Where It's Been and Where It's Going *published in 2010. He is a former partner at investment banking firm Goldman Sachs.*

The financial bailouts of 2008 prompted increased scrutiny of the compensation packages given to Wall Street employees, especially those working for corporations that received federal funds in order to avoid bankruptcy. Although the outcry against those bonuses is somewhat justified, the overall system of compensation is a vital part of the financial industry. Bonuses given to key performers as well as up and coming employees are necessary even during down times in order to retain the best talent in an intensely competitive environment.

1973 was a terrible year on Wall Street. An unexpected crisis in the Middle East led to a quadrupling of oil prices and a serious global economic recession. The president was in serious trouble with Watergate. The S&P 500 index dropped 50%[1] (after 23 years of rising markets), and much of Wall Street fell deeply into the red. There were no profits, and therefore no bonuses.

1. Editor's Note: This figure is incorrect. The S&P 500 index fell 17.5% in 1973.

I was a 35-year-old, nonpartner investment banker then and was horrified to learn that my annual take-home pay would be limited to my small salary, which accounted for about a quarter of my previous year's income. Fortunately the partners decided to pay a small bonus out of their capital that year to help employees like me get by. The next year was no better. Several colleagues with good prospects left the firm and the industry for good. We learned that strong pay-for-performance compensation incentives could cut both ways.

Many wondered if that was still the case last week, when New York State Comptroller Thomas DiNapoli released an estimate that the "securities industry" paid its New York City employees bonuses of $18 billion in 2008, leading to a public outcry. Lost in the denunciations were the powerful benefits of the bonus system, which helped make the U.S. the global leader in financial services for decades. Bonuses are an important and necessary part of the fast-moving, high-pressure industry, and its employees flourish with strong performance incentives.

There is also a fundamental misunderstanding of how bonuses are paid that is further inflaming public opinion. The system has become more complex than most people know, and involves forms of bonuses that are not entirely discretionary.

Bonuses Draw Angry Response

The anger at Wall Street only grew at the news that Merrill Lynch, after reporting $15 billion of losses, had rushed to pay $4 billion in bonuses on the eve of its merger with Bank of America. Because Merrill Lynch and Bank of America were receiving substantial government funds to keep them afloat, the subject became part of the public business. The idea that the banks had paid out taxpayers' funds in undeserved bonuses to employees, together with a leaked report of John Thain's spending $1 million to redecorate his office, understandably provoked a blast of public outrage against Wall Street. The issue was so hot that President Barack Obama interrupted his duties to call the bonuses "shameful" and the "height of irresponsibility." Then, on Wednesday, he announced a new set of rules for those seeking "exceptional" assistance from the Troubled Asset Relief Program [TARP] in the future that would limit cash compensation to $500,000 and restrict severance pay and frills, perks and boondoggles.

Bonuses are an important and necessary part of the fast-moving, high-pressure industry. . . .

In the excitement some of the facts got mixed up. Mr. DiNapoli's estimate included many firms that were not involved with the bailout, and only a few that were. Merrill's actions were approved by its board early in December and consented to by Bank of America. But the basic point is that, despite the dreadful year that Wall Street experienced in 2008, some questionable bonuses were paid to already well-off employees, and that set off the outrage.

Many Americans believe that any bonuses for top executives paid by rescued banks would constitute "excess compensation," a phrase used by Mr. Obama. But no Wall Street CEO taking federal money received a bonus in 2008, and the same was true for most of their senior colleagues. Not only did those responsible receive no bonuses, the value of the stock in their companies paid to them as part of prior-year bonuses dropped by 70% or more, leaving them, collectively, with billions of dollars of unrealized losses.

That's pay for performance, isn't it?

Wall Street Performs Best When Taking Risks

"Wall Street" has always been the quintessential, if ill-defined, symbol of American capitalism. In reality, Wall Street today includes many large banks, investment groups and other institutions, some not even located in the U.S. It has become a euphemism for the global capital markets industry—one in which the combined market value of all stocks and bonds outstanding in the world topped $140 trillion at the end of 2007. Well less than half of the value of this combined market value is represented by American securities, but American banks lead the world in its origination and distribution. Wall Street is one of America's great export industries.

The market thrives on locating new opportunities, providing innovation and a willingness to take risks. It is also, regrettably, subject to what the economist John Maynard Keynes called "animal spirits," the psychological factors that make markets irrational when going up or down. For example, America has enjoyed a bonus it didn't deserve in its freewheeling participation in the housing market, before it became a bubble. Despite great efforts by regulators to manage systemic risk, there have been market failures. The causes of the current market failure, which is the real object of the public anger, go well beyond the Wall Street compensation system—but compensation has been one of them.

The capital-markets industry operates in a very sophisticated and competitive environment, one that responds best to strong performance incentives. People who flourish in this environment are those who want to be paid and advanced based on their individual and their team's performance, and are willing to take the risk that they might be displaced by someone better or that mistakes or downturns may cause them to be laid off or their firms to fail. Indeed, since 1970, 28 major banks or investment banks have failed or been taken up into mergers, and thousands have come and gone into the industry without making much money. Those that have survived the changing fortunes of the industry have done very well—so well, in fact, that they appear to have become symbolic of greedy and reckless behavior.

The Wall Street compensation system has evolved from the 1970s, when most of the firms were private partnerships, owned by partners who paid out a designated share of the firm's profits to nonpartner employees while dividing up the rest for themselves. The nonpartners had to earn their keep every year, but the partners' percentage ownerships in the firms were also reset every year or two. On the whole, everyone's performance was continuously evaluated and rewarded or penalized. The system provided great incentives to create profits, but also, because the partners' own money was involved, to avoid great risk.

Competition for talent made recruitment and retention more difficult and thus tilted negotiating power further in favor of stars.

Competition Is a Double-Edged Sword

The industry became much more competitive when commercial banks were allowed into it. The competition tended to commoditize the basic fee businesses, and drove firms more deeply into trading. As improving technologies created great arrays of new instruments to be traded, the partnerships went public to gain access to larger funding sources, and to spread out the risks of the business. As they did so, each firm tried to maintain its partnership "culture" and compensation system as best it could, but it was difficult to do so.

In time there was significant erosion of the simple principles of the partnership days. Compensation for top managers followed the trend into excess set by other public companies. Competition for talent made recruitment and retention more difficult and thus tilted negotiating power further in favor of stars. Henry Paulson, when he was CEO of Goldman Sachs, once remarked that Wall Street was like other businesses, where 80% of the profits were provided by 20% of the people, but the 20% changed a lot from year to year and market to market. You had to pay everyone well because you never knew what next year would bring, and because there was always someone trying to poach your best trained people, whom you didn't want to lose even if they were not super-stars. Consequently, bonuses in general became more auto-matic and less tied to superior performance. Compensation became the industry's largest expense, accounting for about 50% of net revenues. Warren Buffett, when he was an investor in Salomon Brothers in the late 1980s, once noted that he wasn't sure why anyone wanted to be an investor in a business where management took out half the revenues before share-holders got anything. But be recently invested $5 billion in Goldman Sachs, so he must have gotten over the problem.

As firms became part of large, conglomerate financial in-stitutions, the sense of being a part of a special cohort of similarly acculturated colleagues was lost, and the perfor-mance of shares and options in giant multi-line holding com-panies rarely correlated with an individual's idea of his own performance over time. Nevertheless, the system as a whole worked reasonably well for years in providing rewards for suc-cess and penalties for failures, and still works even in difficult markets such as this one.

At junior levels, bonuses tend to be based on how well the individual is seen to be developing. As employees progress, their compensation is based less on individual performance and more on their role as a manager or team leader. For all professional employees the annual bonus represents a very large amount of the person's take-home pay. At the middle levels, bonuses are set after firm-wide, interdepartmental ne-gotiation sessions that attempt to allocate the firm's compen-sation pool based on a combination of performance and po-tential.

At most firms, much or most of the bonus is paid in stock, which vests over several years, to reward long-term perfor-mance. But the market for talent is competitive and many firms have been compelled to offer guaranteed or minimum bonuses to recruit people, and some star traders have been able to negotiate specific profit-sharing arrangements regardless of what happens to firm-wide profits.

Most of the Wall Street bonuses paid in 2008 were largely directed to those with contracts providing for guaranteed minimums, to those whose efforts during the year contributed to making things better rather than worse, and to middle- and junior-level employees that the firms wanted to retain during difficult times. Last week, reports revealed that UBS, a Swiss bank, hired over 200 experienced brokers in the U.S. in the fourth quarter by offering some "super-sized" bonuses. Even in tough markets, poaching of valuable employees still occurs.

At the senior-most level, in which executives are major shareholders of their firms, all of Wall Street has suffered. The CEOs of Bear Stearns and Lehman Brothers each lost several hundred million dollars as their firms disintegrated. The shares of once-mighty Citigroup, AIG and Bank of America are all now below $6.50 per share [at the time of this writing]. Many top Wall Street executives, including seven CEOs in the U.S. and several more in Europe, have been sacked. Not many other industries have such a harsh, up-or-down compensation system that is so closely tied to performance. The system, of course, is controlled by the firms' boards of directors and approved by their stockholders. If investors don't like it they can vote against it or sell their stock.

Losing key players can be a serious jolt, and despite bear markets there is always another firm willing to hire away the best.

Dynamics Altered When Taxpayer Money Is Used

The entrance of federal funds into the industry, however, has changed things dramatically. For those firms taking TARP money (including some that didn't really want it, and didn't really need it, but had their arms twisted by the Treasury), it is clear that nothing resembling an excess of anything will be permitted. No large cash bonuses, no fancy airplanes or splashy office redecorations.

This is fair enough. Shareholders may be bamboozled into letting these things happen, but taxpayers shouldn't be. Executive compensation paid in stock, especially in difficult times when stock prices are low, offers a strong incentive to turn things around. But the firms will need to be able to run themselves as competitive businesses, offering what it takes to get the best people and teams in place to do what has to be done to return to profitability. Neither the TARP nor Congress should get in the way of doing this. If they do, the most important employees of the firms they are trying to save will seek better situations elsewhere. These businesses are nothing more than their people.

Much of the work on Wall Street is done under great pressure to produce results over short time periods in rapidly changing environments while complying with a myriad of rules and regulations—it isn't for everybody, regardless of brains, personality or motivation. Further, the hierarchy of Wall Street is very flat; people move up quickly based on their ability to seize or create opportunities; everyone wants to be judged on their performance and to be free to rise as far and as fast as they can. Firms made up of such characters generate a lot of energy and initiative, but they also need a lot of supervision and leadership. All are important to the firms' ability to succeed from year to year, especially as markets change. Losing key players can be a serious jolt, and despite bear markets there is always another firm willing to hire away the best.

But the Wall Street bonus system has some serious flaws.

Stricter Regulation Needed to Prevent Future Crises

The most important is the amount of moral hazard that the system creates. Great rewards to executives are paid for successful risk-taking, but the penalties for unsuccessful risk-taking end up being borne by taxpayers. One remedy for this is to charge traders a cost for the capital they use based on the risk that they intend to put it into. Many firms just charge the firm's own cost of the capital, and therefore overstate the profits they record on the riskiest trades. This also overstates the bonuses that should be paid on them.

Another broadly necessary remedy is to subject the entire industry to effective systemic risk regulation, something now being considered by Congress and the administration. They may decide to charge those firms thought to be too big to fail with an insurance premium for taking risks that could affect the whole financial system, similar to the premiums that banks now pay for deposit insurance. Alternatively, a powerful new regulator might be created to be sure that such large banks do not create more systemic risk than they should, by reducing the permissible amount of leverage that banks may use, for instance.

The short-term orientation of the compensation system is another flaw. This needs to be fixed by increasing the proportion of bonuses that reflect performance over a longer term and to provide for "clawbacks" of bonuses accrued when positions or transactions go awry at a later time. Many firms have begun to do this.

Those who criticize Wall Street for excessive compensation may have less to worry about in the future. A recent study by New York University's Thomas Philippon and the University of Virginia's Ariell Reshef of compensation in the U.S. financial services sector since 1909 demonstrates that financial jobs were relatively skill-intensive, complex and highly paid relative to other industries until 1930, and became so again only after 1980, with wages peaking in 1930 and again between 1995 and 2006. They linked the high compensation periods to deregulation, high demand for corporate financial services and increased exposure to credit risk—or in short, to periods of high innovation, bullish markets and extensive trading and risk-taking.

The current financial crisis is very likely to end with new sets of rules that will make it difficult for large banks to continue to operate as if they were hedge funds, by generating systemic risk through large trading positions in active markets. This will result in a change that should moderate bonuses paid by such banks, which they might have to make up for by increasing salaries. It may also encourage a migration of the best and brightest to smaller, less intensely regulated firms such as boutique investment banks, hedge funds or private equity managers.

Public anger is hard to deny, but we shouldn't let it weaken an important industry.

Finally, the controversy over bonuses should remind everyone that a system of free-market capitalism operating inside a vibrant democracy can only succeed if the people accept its benefits and are not offended by what they may perceive (rightly or not) as abusive, greedy or in-your-face behavior. We are less than 10 years away from the last time there was public rage against Wall Street, and to the extent that excessive compensation is part of the problem, the solution is simply to curtail it. But compensation may not be a problem on smaller business platforms that do not involve systemic risk. The larger, complex financial institutions that do involve systemic risk may have to be forced into breaking up into smaller units that don't threaten the whole system.

Still, the people are telling us they're mad as hell and are not going to take it anymore. Public anger is hard to deny, but we shouldn't let it weaken an important industry. Sensible restraints and market forces will cause the industry to reinvent itself. Just has it has done several times since 1973.

7

The Financial Sector Puts Its Own Success Ahead of the Economy

William Black

William Black is a former bank regulator with expertise in white-collar crime, public finance, and regulation. He is also a professor at the University of Missouri and author of the book, The Best Way to Rob a Bank Is to Own One.

The financial sector is supposed to function as a middleman in facilitating the flow of capital through the real economy. Instead it has evolved into a parasitic profiteer and has crippled growth and innovation throughout the world economy. The financial and political power of the largest financial firms has grown so much that reform has proven difficult if not impossible. While economic reform needs to occur within the financial sector, America must also focus on repairing the real economy by working to provide everyone with sustainable jobs and incomes, which is the only way to break the cycle of reoccurring financial crises.

The finance sector's sole function is supplying capital efficiently to aid the real economy. It is a tool to help those that make real tools, not an end in itself.

1. The financial sector harms the real economy.

The financial sector, even when it is not in crisis, harms the real economy. First, it is vastly too large. The finance sector is an intermediary (a "middleman") and like all middlemen it should be as small as possible while still being capable of accomplishing its mission. If it larger than that minimum size it is inherently parasitical. Unfortunately, it is vastly larger than necessary. The finance sector dwarves the real economy that it is supposed to serve. Forty-years ago, our real economy grew better with a financial sector that received one-twentieth as large a percentage of total profits (2%) than does the current financial sector (40%). The minimum measure of how much damage the bloated, grossly over-compensated finance sector causes to the real economy is this massive increase in the share of total national income wasted through the finance sector's parasitism.

The current is only the latest in a long list of economic crises caused by the financial sector.

Second, the finance sector is worse than parasitic. [American economist] James Galbraith's recent book, *The Predator State*, aptly names the problem. The finance sector functions as the sharp canines that the predator state uses to rend the nation. In addition to siphoning off capital for its own benefit, the finance sector misallocates the remaining capital in ways that harm the real economy in order to reward already rich financial elites harming the nation.

- Corporate stock repurchases and grants of stock to officers have exceeded new capital raised by the U.S. capital markets this decade. That means that the capital markets decapitalize the real economy. Too often, they do so in order to enrich corrupt corporate insiders through accounting fraud or backdated stock options.

- The U.S. real economy suffers from critical shortages of employees with strong mathematical, engineering, and scientific backgrounds. Graduates in these three fields all too frequently choose careers in finance rather than the real economy because the financial sector provides far greater executive compensation. Individuals with these quantitative backgrounds work overwhelmingly in devising the financial models that were important contributors to the financial crisis. We take individuals that could be conducting the research & development work essential to the success of our real economy (including its success in becoming sustainable) and put them instead in financial sector activities where, because of that sector's perverse incentives, they further damage the financial sector and the real economy. Michael Moore makes this point in *Capitalism: A Love Story.*

- The financial sector's fixation on accounting earnings leads it to pressure U.S manufacturing and service firms to export jobs abroad, to deny capital to firms that are unionized, and to encourage firms to use foreign tax havens to evade paying U.S. taxes.

- It misallocates capital by creating recurrent financial bubbles. Capital flows not to where it will be most useful to the real economy, but rather to the investments that create the greatest fraudulent accounting gains. The finance sector is particularly prone to providing exceptional amounts of funds to the worst accounting "control frauds." (A control fraud is a seemingly legitimate entity used by the person that controls it as a fraud "weapon." Financial control frauds' "weapon of choice" is accounting fraud.) Accounting control frauds are so attractive to lenders and investors because they produce record, guaranteed short-term accounting "profits." They optimize by growing rapidly like other Ponzi schemes, making loans to borrowers unlikely to be able to repay them (once the bubble bursts), and engaging in extreme leverage. Unless there is effective regulation and prosecutions this misallocation creates an epidemic of accounting control fraud that hyper inflates financial bubbles. The FBI [Federal Bureau of Investigation] began warning of an "epidemic" of mortgage fraud in its congressional testimony in September 2004. It also reports that 80% of mortgage fraud losses come when lender personnel are involved in the fraud. (The other 20% of the fraud would have been impossible had these fraudulent lenders not suborned their underwriting systems and their internal and external controls in order to maximize their growth of bad loans.)

- Because the financial sector cares almost exclusively about high accounting yields and "profits" it misallocates capital away from firms and entrepreneurs that could best improve the real economy (e.g., by reducing short-term profits through funding the expensive research & development that can produce innovative goods and superior sustainability) and could best reduce poverty and inequality (e.g., through microcredit finance that would put the "Payday lenders" and predatory mortgage lenders out of business).

- It misallocates capital by securing enormous governmental subsidies for financial firms, particularly those that have the greatest political power and would otherwise fail due to incompetence and fraud.

2. The financial sector produces recurrent, intensifying economic crises here and abroad.

The current crisis is only the latest in a long list of economic crises caused by the financial sector. When it is not regulated and policed effectively the financial sector produces and hyper inflates bubbles that cause severe economic crises. The current crisis, absent massive, global governmental bailouts, would have caused the catastrophic failure of the global economy. The financial sector has become far more instable since this crisis began as they used their lobbying power to convince Congress to gimmick the accounting rules to hide their massive losses and [U.S. Treasury] Secretary [Timothy] Geithner has declared that the largest financial institutions are exempt from receivership regardless of their insolvency. These factors greatly increase the likelihood that these systemically dangerous institutions (SDIs) will cause a global financial crisis.

3. The financial sector's parasitism is so extraordinary that the finance sector now drives the upper one percent of our nation's income distribution and has driven much of the increase in our grotesque income inequality.

4. The financial sector's parasitism and its leading role in committing and aiding and abetting accounting control fraud combine to:

- Corrupt financial elites and professionals, and

- Spur a rise in Social Darwinism in an attempt to justify the elites' power and wealth. . . .

As financial sector elites became obscenely wealthy through parasitism and fraud their psychological incentives to embrace Social Darwinism surged. While they were by any objective measure the worst elements of the public, their sycophants in the media and the recipients of their political and charitable contributions worshiped them as heroic. Finance CEOs adopted and spread this myth—they were smarter, harder working, and innovative. They rose to the top entirely through their own brilliance and willingness to embrace risk. All of their employees weren't simply above average—they were exceptional. They hated collectivism and adored [author and philosopher] Ayn Rand.

5. The CEO's of the largest financial firms are so powerful that they pose a critical risk to the financial sector, the real economy, and our democracy.

The CEOs can directly, through the firm, and by "bundling" contributions of its officers and employees, easily make enormous political contributions and use their PR [public relations] firms and lobbyists to manipulate the media and public officials. The ability of the financial sector to block meaningful reform after bringing the world to the brink of a second great depression proves how exceptional its powers are to corrupt nearly every critical sector of American public and economic life. The five largest U.S. banks control roughly half of all bank assets. The largest banks use their political and financial power to provide them with competitive advantages that allow them to dominate smaller banks.

This excessive power was a major contributor to the ongoing crisis. Effective financial and securities regulation was anathema to their CEO's ideology (and the greatest danger to their frauds, wealth, and power) and they successfully set out to destroy it. That produced a "criminogenic environment" that prompted the epidemic of accounting control fraud that hyper inflated the housing bubble.

The financial industry's power and progressive corruption combined to produce the perfect white-collar crimes. They successfully lobbied politicians to legalize the obscenity of "dead peasants' insurance" that Michael Moore exposes in chilling detail. State legislatures changed the law to allow a pure tax scam to subsidize large corporations at the expense of their taxpayers.

Caution: Never Forget the Need to Fix the Real Economy

Economic reform efforts are focused almost entirely on fixing finance because the finance sector is so badly broken that it produces recurrent, intensifying crises. The latest crisis brought us to the point of global catastrophe, so the focus on finance is obviously rational. The focus on finance carries a grave risk. The sole purpose of finance is to aid the real economy. The real economy is what creates the goods and services, our jobs, and our incomes. Our ultimate focus needs to be on the real economy. The real economy came off the rails at least three decades ago for the great majority of Americans. We need to commit to fixing the real economy by guaranteeing that everyone willing to work can work and making the real economy sustainable rather than recurrently causing global environmental crises. We must not spend virtually all of our reform efforts on the finance sector and assume that if we solve its defects we will have solved the other fundamental reasons why the real economy has remained so dysfunctional for decades. We need to be work simultaneously to fix finance and the real economy.

8

Tax Evasion Is Easy for Wealthy Big Businesses

Joe Conason

Joe Conason is national correspondent for the New York Observer, *where he writes a weekly column distributed by Creators Syndicate. He is also a columnist for Salon.com.*

Offshore tax havens provide major corporations with the means to conceal assets and avoid paying taxes. The money lost to governments and countries through this practice is staggering, but has attracted far less attention than the bonuses paid out to Wall Street employees in the aftermath of the 2008 financial crisis. Now more than ever the world's most powerful governments should demand accountability from their smaller counterparts, and recoup lost tax monies to aid in their economic recovery.

The popular urge to claw back the bogus bonuses paid by American International Group [AIG] is irresistible and fully justified, but should the Treasury someday retrieve every single bonus dollar, that total of $165 million will make no difference to anyone except a few disgruntled traders. From the jaded perspective of the financiers, the uproar over the AIG bonuses may provide a welcome distraction from far more important (and lucrative) abuses in the world's offshore tax havens.

So rather than continue arguing over chump change, it is long past time for the United States, with its international

Joe Conason, "AIG Is Chump Change—Let's Find Corporate America's Hidden Billions" Salon.com, March 23, 2009. This article first appeared in Salon.com. An online version remains in the Salon archives. Reprinted with permission.

friends and allies, to demand accountability from the long list of tiny countries and principalities, from Andorra and the Cayman Islands to Singapore and Switzerland, where corporations, wealthy clients and unrepentant evildoers hide their assets.

The big claw-back will reach into quaint islands and mountainous principalities, because the same banks, hedge funds and private equity firms responsible for the world financial meltdown keep their profits in those "secrecy spaces"—alongside the ill-gotten gains of numerous drug dealers, dictators and delinquents of every description.

A Common Practice

According to the Government Accountability Office [GAO], *nearly all of America's top 100 corporations maintain subsidiaries* in countries identified as tax havens. As the GAO notes, there could be reasons other than avoiding the IRS [Internal Revenue Service] to set up branches in places such as Singapore, Luxembourg and Switzerland, where taxes are light or nonexistent and keeping clients' illicit secrets is considered a matter of national pride.

But what reason other than evasion could there be for Goldman Sachs Group to set up three subsidiaries in Bermuda, five in Mauritius, and 15 in the Cayman Islands? Why did Countrywide Financial need two subsidiaries in Guernsey? Why did Wachovia need 18 subsidiaries in Bermuda, three in the British Virgin Islands, and 16 in the Caymans? Why did Lehman Brothers need 31 subsidiaries in the Caymans? What do Bank of America's 59 subsidiaries in the Caymans actually do? Why does Citigroup need 427 separate subsidiaries in tax havens, including 12 in the Channel Islands, 21 in Jersey, 91 in Luxembourg, 19 in Bermuda and 90 in the Caymans? What exactly is going on at Morgan Stanley's 19 subs in Jersey, 29 subs in Luxembourg, 14 subs in the Marshall Islands, and its amazing 158 subs in the Caymans? And speaking of AIG, why does it have 18 subs in tax-haven countries? (Don't expect to find out from Fox News Channel or the *New York Post*, because News Corp. has its own constellation of strange subsidiaries, including 33 in the Caymans alone.)

[N]early all of America's top 100 corporations maintain subsidiaries in countries identified as tax havens.

When the cost of these shenanigans was last estimated two years ago, the U.S. government's annual loss in revenue due to tax avoidance by major corporations and super-rich individuals was pegged at about $100 billion—considerably more than a rounding error, even today. But of course that is only a rough assessment, as is the estimate of $12 trillion in untaxed assets hidden around the world. Nobody will know for certain until the books are opened and transparency is established.

Whatever the accurate accounting proves to be, it is certain to exceed hundreds of billions annually worldwide. That is money every country will need badly for years, to repay debt, finance reconstruction, and fund services, as the world economy struggles to revive itself. Even in the developing countries, where incomes are much lower and billionaires tend to be scarce, the annual revenue loss could be as much as $50 billion—enough to meet the U.N.'s Millennium Development Goals (if only the money were not stolen by local elites and wired away to numbered accounts in tax havens).

Little Risk of Prosecution

None of these tax havens could exist without the connivance or at least the cooperation of the world's most powerful governments, which remain dominated by financial industry lobbyists even now. The Organization for Economic Cooperation and Development [OECD] has sought greater transparency from the tax havens for years, hearing promises from most and defiance from a few.

But in reality almost nothing was accomplished until last year, when U.S. law enforcement authorities began to pursue Union Bank of Switzerland (UBS) executives with criminal indictments. The UBS probe led to a settlement last month [in February 2009] that included a fine of $780 million and an agreement to provide information about tens of thousands of American clients maintaining secret accounts at that huge bank.

Congress and the White House should . . . make breaking the tax havens a high priority.

Over the past several years, however, the trend has gone the other way, with abuse of bank secrecy and the expatriation of investment and profits growing rapidly. On the tiny island of Jersey in the English Channel, for instance, the authorities responded to political pressure from hedge funds, which have placed more than $80 billion in deposits there, by establishing a "zero regulation regime" last year that literally removed all restrictions and reporting on financial transactions. Jersey's counterparts in Guernsey and the Cayman Islands responded by assuring the hedge funds that they, too, would consider abolishing all regulation.

Perhaps the UBS case indicates a change in that unwholesome trend and a renewed willingness on the part of American authorities to crack the tax havens—which was not a priority, to put it mildly, of the [George W.] Bush administration. As a senator, Barack Obama supported legislation to break open the secret financial regimes, by retaliating against countries and principalities that refuse to cooperate. Now Congress and the White House should pass such legislation and make breaking the tax havens a high priority in partnership with the European Union, the OECD and World Bank. They could start by threatening to outlaw transactions between American banks and financial institutions in any country that rejects new rules for transparency and reciprocal information.

If Americans want to make the authors of our misery pay up, then the auditors must go where the money is, as [bank robber] Willie Sutton might have explained—and take hundreds of billions back.

The Health Insurance Industry Is Guilty of Deceiving Customers

Alice Gomstyn

Alice Gomstyn is a business reporter for ABC News. Prior to joining ABC News in 2008, she worked as an education reporter and blogger at the Journal News *in New York.*

Former Cigna senior executive Wendell Potter along with several other healthcare experts testified at Senate hearings as Congress sought to address the growing crisis surrounding healthcare concerns in America. Health insurance companies regularly place profits over healthcare. Canceled policies, denied claims, and the growing cost of insurance premiums have made more Americans vulnerable to financial ruin and health setbacks even in cases where they purchased what they thought to be adequate insurance coverage.

Frustrated Americans have long complained that their insurance companies valued the all-mighty buck over their health care. Today, a retired insurance executive confirmed their suspicions, arguing that the industry that once employed him regularly rips off its policyholders.

"[T]hey confuse their customers and dump the sick, all so they can satisfy their Wall Street investors," former Cigna senior executive Wendell Potter said during a hearing on health insurance today before the Senate Committee on Commerce, Science, and Transportation.

Potter, who has more than 20 years of experience working in public relations for insurance companies Cigna and Humana, said companies routinely drop seriously ill policyholders so they can meet "Wall Street's relentless profit expectations."

"They look carefully to see if a sick policyholder may have omitted a minor illness, a pre-existing condition, when applying for coverage, and then they use that as justification to cancel the policy, even if the enrollee has never missed a premium payment," Potter said. ". . . (D)umping a small number of enrollees can have a big effect on the bottom line."

[T]hey confuse their customers and dump the sick, all so they can satisfy their Wall Street investors. . .

Small businesses, in particular, he said, have had trouble maintaining their employee health insurance coverage, he said.

"All it takes is one illness or accident among employees at a small business to prompt an insurance company to hike the next year's premiums so high that the employer has to cut benefits, shop for another carrier, or stop offering coverage altogether," he said.

Potter also faulted insurance companies for being misleading both in advertising their policies to new customers and in communicating with existing policyholders.

More and more people, he said, are falling victim to "deceptive marketing practices" that encourage them to buy "what essentially is fake insurance," policies with high costs but surprisingly limited benefits.

Insurance companies continue to mislead consumers through "explanation of benefits" documents that note what payments the insurance company made and what's left for consumers to pay out of pocket, Potter said.

The documents, he said, are "notoriously incomprehensible."

"Insurers know that policyholders are so baffled by those notices they usually just ignore them or throw them away. And that's exactly the point," he said. "If they were more understandable, more consumers might realize that they are being ripped off."

Potter did have some kind words to share about his former employer, Cigna.

"I hope that I'm not coming across as someone who's critical of my former employer. I had a good career at Cigna and was well-compensated. I was there for 15 years and lasted 15 years," he said. "My comments are directed toward an industry that is really going in the wrong direction and taking this country in the wrong direction."

In a statement released this evening, Cigna said that it "strongly disagree(s) with the suggestion that, motivated by profits, the insurance industry has deliberately attempted to confuse or unfairly treat covered individuals."

The company said it has a team dedicated to help its policyholders understand their benefits and that it is advocating for improvements to the health care system, including mandated coverage for all.

The Senate also heard from Karen Pollitz, a research professor at the Georgetown University Health Policy Institute, and Nancy Metcalf, a senior program editor at Consumer Reports.

Pollitz said that insurance companies should provide more information about how coverage works so that consumers are better equipped to compare policies as they shop for coverage.

Metcalf spoke of how many Americans have mistakenly bought lower-cost insurance policies without realizing how little the policies actually cover.

"They were no match for insurance companies who know exactly how to design and market plans whose gaping holes don't become apparent until it's much, much too late," she said.

Sick Patients, Canceled Policies

As Congress and the White House continue to work on health-care reform, health insurance companies have been subject to intense grilling by lawmakers during several hearings.

Last week, three insurance company executives testified before Congress on the issue of health insurance rescissions—the cancellation of insurance policies—for seriously ill policy-holders.

A year-long investigation by a subcommittee of the House Committee on Energy and Commerce found that three major U.S. insurance companies, WellPoint Inc., Assurant Health and United HealthGroup, canceled nearly 19,800 customer policies between 2003 and 2007.

The companies argue that rescissions are relatively rare and are important in combatting insurance fraud.

"In 2008, WellPoint's affiliated health plans rescinded one-tenth of one percent of new individual market enrollment," WellPoint said in an e-mailed statement to ABCNews.com. "While rescissions impact a very small percentage of applicants for coverage it is important to protect the majority who are honest on their applications for coverage."

Insurance companies are, by law, allowed to rescind policies for customers who are found to have purposely lied or omitted information from their policy applications. But some of the rescissions the subcommittee found were for seriously ill people who had simply made mistakes on their applications.

Catching Fraud or Skirting Health Care Bills?

The committee found that the companies saved more than $300 million as a result of the rescissions. One WellPoint employee, the committee said, was awarded with a perfect performance appraisal after saving the company $10 million. (WellPoint told ABCNews.com that the money-saving reference in the appraisal was an "aberration" and said that the employee did not receive any extra salary or bonus.)

"These practices reveal that when an insurance company receives a claim for an expensive, life-saving treatment, some of them will look for a way, any way, to avoid having to pay for it," subcommittee chairman Rep. Bart Stupak, D-Mich., said at the hearing.

Two former customers of Blue Cross of California, a subsidiary of WellPoint Inc., told ABCNews.com that the company canceled their insurance policies after such mistakes.

Mark Robison, of Santa Rosa, Calif., said Blue Cross canceled his policy after claiming that he knowingly omitted information about his then 8-year-old son having an undescended testicle. Robison said that Blue Cross already had information on his son's medical history on file. His son was under Blue Cross's coverage when he was initially diagnosed with his condition.

Sally Marrara, of Los Angeles, said the company canceled her policy after determining she never told them about back pain and a history of anti-depressant use. Marrara said the back pain was related to a hysterectomy that she had included in her Blue Cross application, while the anti-depressant use dated back some 10 years. She used the drugs temporarily, she said, to cope with her father's death.

Both Robison, whose son eventually underwent surgery, and Marrara, who was later diagnosed with lupus, are now saddled with thousands in medical bills. Each is suing the company.

"It's a total travesty," Robison said. "It's unwarranted and unconscionable."

Insurance companies argue that health care reforms that ensure coverage for those with pre-existing conditions should help tackle the problem of rescissions.

Health insurance companies are forcing consumers to pay more than they should.

"In a reformed health care system, individuals and families will never again have to worry that they may lose coverage on the basis of their medical history," Karen Ignagni, the president of the health insurance company lobbying group America's Health Insurance Plans, wrote in a letter to Stupak.

Out-of-Network Agony

Today's Senate hearing comes three months after the Senate held hearings on concerns that health insurance companies are forcing consumers to pay more than they should for care from doctors outside the companies' networks.

The March hearings included testimony from a representative of the New York State Attorney General's office. An investigation by the state attorney general found that the insurance industry systematically under-estimates how much it should reimburse policyholders.

UnitedHealth Group CEO Stephen J. Hemsley said at a March 31 hearing that the insurance company stands by the integrity of the database—run by UnitedHealth subsidiary Ingenix—used to determine reimbursements and health care costs.

A report released today by the Senate Commerce Committee found that in addition to UnitedHealth, at least 17 other major insurance companies used Ingenix data.

The committee has claimed that evidence indicates that Ingenix data is faulty—a claim the company has denied.

10

There Is a Crisis of Morality Among Investors

Christopher Grey

Christopher Grey is a cofounder and chief financial and operational officer of CapLinked, a collaborative network for private companies, investors, and their advisers. He is a frequent contributor to thestreet.com.

Warnings about the possible illegality of Bernie Madoff's investments were easy to find. Yet investors still poured money into his funds and held onto the belief that he could somehow beat the odds. This mindset is emblematic of an entitlement mentality that is prevalent in America today. Aided by increasingly lax regulations, people and corporations no longer see anything wrong with cheating to get what they feel they deserve. The country needs to change course and once again honor the concepts of honesty and hard work that made this nation great.

Maybe I was raised differently from the super rich on Wall Street or in Palm Beach, but in my world stealing is not a "tragedy"—it's a crime.

I keep reading that many people, mostly insiders from enclaves of extreme wealth and privilege, are calling Bernard Madoff's implosion a "tragedy." This actually sickens me because it exposes just how serious the crisis of morality is among America's elites.

It is not a "tragedy" to me that so many people with so much money and privilege were suckered by someone like

Christopher Grey, "Madoff Implosion Is No 'Tragedy'" thestreet.com, December 16, 2008. Copyright © 2008 by Wrights Media. Reproduced by permission.

Madoff. I think it is just a combination of laziness, stupidity and greed. That is not tragic to me. It is pathetic.

Madoff was making 1% per month, year after year with no losses and nobody else on Wall Street or anywhere could explain his returns. Even Madoff didn't explain it.

Plenty of people openly told the SEC [Securities and Exchange Commission] and the media that he had to be either running a Ponzi scheme or doing something else illegally. Nevertheless, so many of these "sophisticated" investors piled their money into his fund. Many of them invested a huge percentage of their personal net worth, charitable trust, inheritance or future bequests to their heirs. What were they thinking?

It is not a "tragedy" to me that so many people with so much money and privilege were suckered by someone like [Bernie] Madoff.

Many were just following their friends. Many were lazy. Many were stupid. Many were greedy. None of them stopped to think that Madoff's returns were literally impossible unless he was doing something illegal.

Personally, I have no sympathy for Madoff's investors or their heirs or dependents or anyone who believes that they are entitled to get something for nothing in life. That is a philosophy of losers and apparently also of many of America's so-called elites.

Investors Expected Something for Nothing

This is very sad and, in my opinion, symbolizes exactly what is wrong with this country and why we're in so much trouble right now. America has a crisis of morality created by the undeserved and abused privilege at the top of our society that has trickled down to the middle and lower classes who also want to "get theirs" without earning it.

The same perverse mentality that causes these Madoff investors to expect a free lunch compels working people to believe that they don't need to work and save to buy things that they want. They can just go borrow the money, and if they can't pay it back, so what? They can just default and hope either their relatives or friends or the government will bail them out. Or they just declare bankruptcy.

Many American companies and their executives have the same thought process. Borrow as much as you can, make any stupid investment that comes across your desk—especially if the people promoting it are your friends—pay yourself and your friends as much as possible while the getting is good, and then go beg the government and investors and lenders for help when things go bad.

These financial and corporate leaders want to stick the honest taxpayers or investors or lenders or our foreign creditors with the bill for their greed, laziness and stupidity. If the government or others won't bail them out, they just go bankrupt, screw their creditors and destroy all the jobs and retirement savings of the company's hard-working employees.

This has become a way of life in America, and it is destroying our country. At its most basic level, there is no longer such a thing as honor in America.

In most other advanced societies, especially in Asia, the higher up you are in society, the more you are expected to behave within a certain set of rules. Those rules are mostly about honor and taking responsibility for your behavior and trying to set an example for people lower on the socioeconomic ladder.

Of course, there are frauds and crooks and other varieties of evil-doers in every society. But in most other advanced societies, these people are publicly despised and humiliated and punished swiftly and surely to such an extent that it serves as a strong deterrent to this kind of behavior.

In America, not only does our extremely lax and often nonexistent regulation make it ridiculously easy to get away with fraud and other white-collar crimes, but our justice system make it easy for criminals with money to delay and often escape justice entirely.

Even worse, there is actually a celebrity factor and some kind of respect in America for frauds who get away with it and "beat the system."

It is not unusual in Asia for elites who are exposed as frauds to commit suicide. Why? It is because of the dishonor. I'm not holding my breath for Bernie Madoff or [Lehman Brother's CEO] Dick Fuld or [Countrywide Financial CEO] Angelo Mozilo to do that. There's a great line from the movie *Mississippi Burning*, when Gene Hackman's character says: "Rattlesnakes don't commit suicide." I think that pretty much says it all about America's morally bankrupt elites.

How do we look to the rest of the world? If you were an Asian investor watching all of this, what would you think of investing in America after recent events? I think they are probably disgusted with us.

It was reported without much publicity in the past few weeks that the Chinese have announced they will not make any more investments in U.S. financial companies. I think this is just the beginning of what we have in store for us in the years to come. As foreign investors, especially in Asia, become increasingly repulsed by our ethics as well as our poor judgment, they will vote with their wallets and stop investing so much money here. They cannot completely get out because we are too big, but we need to keep their money flowing in every day just to keep the lights on in our economy.

American Leaders Must Promote Change from the Top

Our whole country is teetering on the brink of an enormous amount of debt and a lack of sustainable income to service that debt. In the short run, the government will try to print as many dollars as possible and issue as many bonds as possible to fill the gap. However, in the long run we need to generate more income, save more domestically, or get foreigners to keep investing more money here.

So far we are not doing anything material to improve our chances of succeeding with any of these alternatives. We're not making the situation any better by reducing our interest rates to levels that are no longer attractive even to the Japanese. . . .

I do not own any stocks, but I am not short any stocks either. The goal for conservative investors right now, in my opinion, is to position yourself for the significant likelihood that the U.S. economy, and to a lesser extent the entire world economy, faces a cataclysmic adjustment away from a growth model based on leverage and Ponzi finance.

This will either cause severe deflation, which is why you need a lot of cash, or it will cause severe inflation if the government successfully prints enough money, which is why you need some ways to hedge your cash by shorting Treasuries and owning gold and silver. I do not own foreign currencies because I think the gold and silver are better and also because I think ultimately all paper currencies will follow the dollar in order to stay competitive.

America has been given a lot of rope in the form of cheap and easy money for too long.

I don't have confidence in most other highly liquid and easily accessible investments for individuals until our financial and other leaders in America learn the meaning of honor and start taking this country down a path of working, saving, investing and producing rather than borrowing, spending, stealing and defaulting.

This change needs to come from the top. It is particularly important that the new Obama administration avoid scandal and get serious about financial regulation and enforcement of securities laws against frauds and crooks. This is essential to restore confidence of investors both domestically and overseas.

America has been given a lot of rope in the form of cheap and easy money for too long, and we have used it to hang ourselves financially and morally.

We need to start getting our house in order, get back to basics and change the direction of this country if we're going to sustain the great legacy that we've built during the past 300 years.

11

Outrageous Fraud Is Widespread in the Mortgage Industry

Zach Carter

Zach Carter is the economics editor for Alternet. *He is a fellow at Campaign for America's Future, writes a weekly blog on the economy for the* Media Consortium, *and is a frequent contributor to* The Nation *magazine.*

Washington Mutual displayed a stunningly brazen form of fraudulent activity before its collapse in September of 2008. The company and its executives actively pushed risky mortgage products on their clients knowing that a crisis involving these loans was imminent. But a weak regulatory system shares equal blame for allowing the firm to start down this fraudulent road in the first place. The repeal of the Glass-Steagall law in 1999 which prohibited the mixing of Wall Street security trading activities with regular bank business, set the stage for Washington Mutual and other fraudulent companies to deceive homeowners and precipitate the country's mortgage crisis.

There are two types of financial outrages: acts that are outrageously illegal, and acts that are, outrageously, legal. Yesterday's [April 13, 2010] Senate hearing on the rise and fall of Washington Mutual [WaMu] was a rare examination of the former outrage, documenting the pervasive practice of fraud at every level of the now-defunct bank's business.

All of Washington Mutual's sketchy practices can be traced back to rampant fraud in its mortgage lending offices. The company repeatedly performed internal audits of its lending practices, and discovered multiple times that enormous proportions of the loans it was issuing were based on fraudulent documents. At some offices, the fraud rate was on new mortgages over 70%, and at yesterday's hearing, the company's former Chief Risk Officer James Vanasek described its mortgage fraud as "systemic."

When most people think of mortgage fraud, they think of a clever borrower conning an unwitting banker into extending him a loan he cannot afford. But this isn't really how fraud usually works in the mortgage business. According to the FBI [Federal Bureau of Investigation], 80% of mortgage fraud is committed by the lender, so it shouldn't be surprising that WaMu's internal audits concluded that its widespread fraud was being "willfully" perpetrated by its own employees. The company also engaged in textbook predatory lending across all of its mortgage lending activities—issuing loans based on the value of the property, while ignoring the borrower's ability to repay the loan.

Securitization is immensely profitable . . . it allows banks to dump risky mortgages off their books at a profit.

These findings alone are pretty bad stuff in the world of white-collar crime. For several years, WaMu was engaged in fraudulent lending, WaMu managers knew it was engaged in fraudulent lending, and didn't stop it. The company was setting up thousands, if not millions of borrowers for foreclosure, while booking illusory short-term profits and paying out giant bonuses for its employees and executives. During the housing boom, WaMu Chairman and CEO Kerry Killinger took home between $11 million and $20 million every single year, much of it "earned" on outright fraud.

WaMu Ignored Its Own Audits

But the WaMu scandal gets much worse. WaMu is routinely referred to as a pure mortgage lender, one whose simple business model can be contrasted with the complex wheelings and dealings of Wall Street titans like Lehman Brothers and Bear Stearns. That characterization is grossly inaccurate. WaMu was very heavily engaged in the business of packaging mortgages into securities and marketing them to investors. This is a core investment banking function, something ordinary mortgage banks like WaMu were legally barred from engaging in until 1999, when Congress repealed the Glass-Steagall Act, a critical Depression-era reform.

Securitization is immensely profitable, and under the right circumstances, it allows banks to dump risky mortgages off their books at a profit. That's exactly what WaMu did. Even after internal audits flagged specific loans as fraudulent, WaMu's securitization shop still went ahead and packaged those exact same loans into securities, and sold them to investors. Knowingly peddling fraudulent securities is a straightforward act of securities fraud, one made all the more severe by the fact that WaMu never told its investors it had sold them securities full of fraudulent loans. The only question now is whether anyone will be personally held accountable for the act.

So far, we've got fraud on fraud—but wait! The WaMu saga actually gets worse still. When the mortgage market started falling apart, WaMu ordered a study on the likelihood that one if its riskiest mortgage products, the option-ARM [Adjustable Rate Mortgage] loan, would begin defaulting en masse. The report concluded that, indeed, option-ARMs were about to default like crazy, within a matter of months. Option-ARMs feature a low introductory monthly payment for a few years, often so low that borrowers actually end up going deeper into debt, despite making their regular payments. After a few years, the monthly payment increases dramatically—sometimes by as much as 400 percent. Suddenly this cheap loan is outrageously unaffordable, and if home prices decline, borrowers are immediately headed for foreclosure.

Imminent Defaults Only Made WaMu Sell More Risky Products

Now, most would-be homeowners are not very interested in this kind of loan. It seems dangerous, because it *is* dangerous. So WaMu actively coached its loan officers to persuade skeptical borrowers into accepting this predatory garbage instead of an ordinary mortgage.

This assault on its own borrowers is only half of WaMu's option-ARM hustle. For a while, Wall Street investors really liked option-ARMs. They were inherently risky, which meant they were much more profitable, if you ignored the risk that they might someday default, and Wall Street was all too happy to engage in this kind of creative accounting.

But when WaMu conducted its study on looming option-ARM defaults, the prospect of heavy, imminent losses did not convince the company to abandon the business. Instead, WaMu began issuing as many option-ARMs as it could. The idea was to jam as many of these loans into its securitization machine as it could before investors decided to stop buying option-ARM securities altogether.

That means WaMu was knowingly setting up both borrowers and investors for a fall. The company was actually trying to extend loans that it *knew* would be disastrous for its borrowers—and then selling them to investors that it *knew* would end up taking heavy losses. Whether or not this constitutes illegal fraud will depend on some technicalities, but it is clearly an act of outrageous deception.

When the securitization markets finally froze up, WaMu got stuck with billions in terrible, terrible loans it had issued, and the company failed spectacularly. One of the few good calls the U.S. government made during the financial crisis was the decision not to extend bailout funds to WaMu, not to save the jobs of its executives, and to allow the company to fail. It was seized by the FDIC [Federal Deposit Insurance Corporation] in late September 2008, and immediately sold to J.P. Morgan Chase, at no cost to taxpayers.

Regulation Needs to Put Consumers First

But WaMu's story is nevertheless rife with implications here for Wall Street reform. First, regulation matters. Everything WaMu did could have been stopped not only by an engaged regulator who worried about the company's bottom line, but by a regulator who cared about consumer protection in any degree whatsoever. WaMu's regulator, the Office of Thrift Supervision, didn't care about either, but it was particularly uninterested in consumer protection rules, because those often conflict with bank profitability. If we establish a new regulator that is charged only with writing and enforcing consumer protection rules, it won't worry about how profitable consumer predation might be, it will simply crack down on it. In the process, it could actually protect the company's bottom line.

One of the few good calls the U.S. government made during the financial crisis was the decision . . . [to] allow the company to fail.

Second, at yesterday's [April 13, 2010] hearing, former WaMu Chief Risk Officer James Vanasek acknowledged that his bank would not have been able to wreak so much economic destruction without the repeal of Glass-Steagall, which barred any mixing between complex Wall Street securities dealings and ordinary, plain-vanilla banking. He even went so far as to offer a tepid endorsement for reinstating the law.

A lot of predatory mortgage firms didn't run their own securitization shops—they sold their loans directly to Wall Street firms, which handled the securitization on their own. So proponents of the Glass-Steagall repeal (most of them employed at one point or another by a major banking conglomerate) argue that the crisis would have occurred with or without the repeal. That argument is basically a distraction, as the WaMu case reveals. Over the course of just a few years, WaMu's entire mortgage banking operation transformed from a boring, profitable, plain-vanilla enterprise, into a feeding trough for its risky securitization activities. There is simply no way that transformation could have occurred without the lure of easy in-house securitization profits. It is possible to conceive of a mortgage crisis taking place without the repeal of Glass-Steagall, but it is utterly impossible to imagine a mortgage crisis as severe as the one we are still living through.

It will be very surprising if criminal charges are not soon filed against some of WaMu's former executives. But WaMu isn't the only bad actor from the financial crisis. This is basically how the entire U.S. mortgage market operated for at least five years. Dozens of lenders who are still active, many of them saved by generous taxpayer bailouts, were engaged in similar activities. There's only one way to churn out billions of dollars worth of lousy mortgages for several years, and it involves a prolonged campaign of fraud and deception.

12

US Contractors Are Responsible for Much of the Corruption in Afghanistan

Iman Hasan

Iman Hasan is a journalist based in the Afghanistan capital city of Kabul. He writes on politics and society.

Afghan officials have been accused of corruption by the US government but the United States appears to be guilty of much of the fraud in Afghanistan. Billions of dollars allocated to the reconstruction of the country are unaccounted for and investigations attribute the loss to waste, fraud, and theft. Large defense contractors such as Raytheon and Lockheed Martin are profiting from the continuation of the Afghan war and very little of the money they receive actually makes its way into reconstruction projects that would help the country regain its capacity to govern itself.

Many Afghans, from government officials and parliamentarians to the common man are disgruntled with US officials relentlessly accusing them of being corrupt—while ignoring their own government's fraud and misappropriations in the $56 billion development budget approved by the Congress for the reconstruction of Afghanistan. Afghans deem the US responsible for corrupting their society.

For [US President Barack] Obama's administration, 'corruption warnings' are a new blackmail tool to use against the

[Afghan president Hamid] Karzai government. There has been constant rhetoric to "eradicate corruption" and "stop misusing US tax payers' money," without realising that only 20% of the allocated funds are at the disposal of the Afghan government while 80% are utilised by the US Department of State, Defence and USAID [United States Agency for International Development]. These three departments rely extensively on private contractors for the implementation of various projects, ranging from reconstruction of Afghanistan, eradicating drugs, training of Afghan security forces and officials and providing security to Nato [North Atlantic Treaty Organization] supply convoys.

Since 2001, the US Congress has appropriated nearly $56 billion for the reconstruction funds of Afghanistan, which cannot be tracked down. It has either been wasted, stolen or abused.

Missing Records

There is absolutely no record of the amount utilised from 2001 to 2006 except for the vague documentation of $17.7 billion spent during the financial year 2007–2009, which only identifies the 7000 contractors hired to implement the projects—but does not evaluate the projects. Therefore, there is no guarantee if the US tax payers' money amounting to $56 billion is fairly spent or abused.

Since 2001, the US Congress has appropriated nearly $56 billion for the reconstruction funds of Afghanistan which cannot be tracked down.

[Former US President George W.] Bush's government after eight years of engagement in Afghanistan established the Office of the Special Inspector General for Afghanistan Reconstruction (SIGAR) in 2008 "to conduct independent and objective audits, inspections, and investigations on the use of taxpayer dollars and related funds":

Even the Office of the Special Inspector General is unable to track down the money spent during 2001 to 2006. It recently released a report on the "waste, fraud and abuse" of $17.7 billion (spent during the financial year 2007–2009) of the total reconstruction fund of $56 billion.

The report is essentially a document holding the US responsible for the corruption in Afghanistan. "The large US investment in Afghanistan remains at risk of being wasted or subject to waste, fraud and abuse," reads the document.

Who Benefits from America's Wars?

65 per cent of the $17.7 billion has been channelled through the Department of Defence, which hired largely those companies who are essentially part of the Military Industrial Complex (MIC). These huge corporations depend mostly or entirely on the Pentagon for their profits and have hugely benefited from the US wars.

It has been a known fact that the Bush-Cheney administration had direct financial interest in these companies. Vice President [Dick] Cheney was the CEO of Halliburton for over five years that profited the most out of the Iraq war.

Some of the largest defense contractors belonging to the Military Industrial Complex hired by the Defence Department, for Afghanistan are DynCorp, Black Water (Xe Services), Lockheed Martin, Northrop Grumman, Raytheon, Louis Berger and Bearing Point.

It is believed that some companies like Lockheed Martin and Raytheon draw close to 100 per cent of their business from defence contracts.

Since last year, more defence contractors belonging to the MIC have been added to the list to benefit from the war in

Afghanistan. Along with the Department of Defence, the State Department also supports the companies belonging to the complex.

These huge corporations depend mostly or entirely on the Pentagon for their profits.

Imagine the billions of dollars DynCorp has earned in the past ten years, considering $1.8 billion it earned in two years from a single project of drug eradication, which was administered by the State Department. DynCorp is involved in multiple projects in Afghanistan.

US wars are largely dictated by the MIC. President [Dwight D.] Eisenhower in his farewell address on 17 January 1961 warned the US nation against this complex to never let it "endanger our liberties or democratic process. We must guard against the acquisition of unwarranted influence, whether sought or unsought, by the military-industrial complex."

The War in Afghanistan Could Have Been Avoided

Several diplomats in Kabul believe that the war in Afghanistan could have been avoided if it wasn't supported by the powers associated with MIC. [The] United States could have followed the policy of "reconciliation and reintegration" in 2001, that it is compelled to follow now. But even now the efforts for the reconciliation with the Taliban are constantly being disrupted by the strategy adopted by the Department of Defence.

As the war-oriented economy brings advantages to some powers in the US, some elements in Afghanistan who oppose reconciliation with the Taliban are benefiting immensely from the situation—living the lavish life style which they couldn't afford otherwise.

Besides the Military Industrial Complex, there is also the intelligence complex which has been playing a greater role in corrupting the Afghan society since 2001, whose billions of dollars of expenditure has never been accounted for.

The intelligence complex's profligate distribution of boxes and suitcases of cash amongst the different segments of Afghan society—Afghan media, NGOs [non-governmental organization] and allegedly government officials—has also encouraged other countries. India is one of the countries which has taken a leaf out of the CIA's [Central Intelligence Agency] book.

Such notorious tactics used by powerful elements of the US system are further deteriorating the Afghan society and undermining the long term goals "to develop governing capacity of Afghans and foster economic development."

Lack of Transparency

This is still not the complete picture of US corruption and lack of oversight of reconstruction funds—meant for achieving long term goals in Afghanistan. There is no transparency even in the salary support provided to the Afghan government employees and technical advisors since 2002. The US government is unable to determine the amount it has been paying, the identity and the total number of recipients. Since the number and identity of the recipients is not clear the salaries can go to anyone in anyone's name.

The audacity of the Obama administration is that with the deteriorating economy and historic unemployment in the US, it has requested an additional $16.2 billion, which would bring the funding for reconstruction of Afghanistan to more than $72 billion.

The additional funds are more likely to be spent to achieve the hidden goals of some powers than the long term 'stated' goals of the US government in Afghanistan[.]

13

Contractor Misbehavior Goes Unpunished

Jeremy Scahill

Jeremy Scahill is an investigative journalist. He is author of the book, Blackwater: The Rise of the World's Most Powerful Mercenary Army *and a frequent contributor to* The Nation *magazine.*

President Barack Obama accepted the resignation of General Stanley McChrystal after the general made derogatory comments about Obama and other administration officials in an article published by Rolling Stone *magazine. But private defense contractor Blackwater has suffered little consequence despite numerous allegations and indictments of wrongdoing ranging from murder to gun smuggling and theft. Rather the company has been awarded new services contracts in 2010 from the US government in the amount of $200 million. The disparity in the treatment of General McChrystal and Blackwater reflects poorly on the Obama administration, which appears more concerned with comments in a magazine than repeated illegal actions on the ground.*

The mercenary firm Blackwater is clearly more teflon than Gen. Stanley McChrystal. While McChrystal sips Bud Light Lime, watching *Talladega Nights* and ponders what private sector job to scoop up, Erik Prince's crusading private

Jeremy Scahill, "Of General Stanley McChrystal and Blackwater" *The Nation*, June 24, 2010. Copyright © 2010 The Nation. All rights reserved. Reproduced by permission.

soldiers will still be running around Afghanistan and other theaters of undeclared US wars globally with the CIA [Central Intelligence Agency]. All with the blessing of the Commander in Chief.

While President Obama sacked McChrystal after comments attributed to him and his inner circle were published in a now infamous [2010] *Rolling Stone* article, Blackwater is being rewarded with new contracts despite its track record of scores of acts of misconduct, including allegations of murdering and manslaughtering civilians, weapons charges, conspiracy and obstruction of justice to name a few.

> *Blackwater is being rewarded with new contracts despite its track record of scores of acts of misconduct.*

Given McChrystal's alleged involvement in the torture of detainees at Camp Nama in Iraq, his primary role in the cover-up of Pat Tillman's death and other dark acts involving his time commanding the Joint Special Operations Command under the Bush-Cheney administration, McChrystal should have never been named commander in Afghanistan. When he was appointed, Obama sent a message about the kind of policy he wanted in Afghanistan—one which favored unaccountable, unattributable direct action forces accustomed to operating in secret and away from effective oversight. Indeed, in the *Rolling Stone* article, McChrystal appeared to admit his famous commitment to decreasing civilian deaths was a sham operation. According to *Rolling Stone*: "'You better be out there hitting four or five targets tonight,' McChrystal will tell a Navy Seal he sees in the hallway at headquarters. Then he'll add, 'I'm going to have to scold you in the morning for it, though.'"

President Obama was right to fire McChrystal (technically he accepted his resignation)—it should have happened long ago. That McChrystal was fired for the *Rolling Stone* article, however, and not for the way he prosecuted the Afghan war speaks volumes about the administration's Afghanistan position and policy vision (not to mention that Dick Cheney's general, David Petraeus, was named as McChrystal's successor).

Contrast Obama's McChrystal treatment with his Blackwater treatment.

Criminal Charges Do Not Deter Contract Awards to Blackwater

In January [2010], two Blackwater operatives were indicted on murder charges stemming from a shooting in Afghanistan in May 2008. In March, Senator Carl Levin, chair of the Senate Armed Services Committee, called on the Justice Department to investigate Blackwater's use of a shell company, Paravant, to win training contracts in Afghanistan. On June 11 federal prosecutors filed a massive brief in their appeal of last year's dismissal by a federal judge of manslaughter charges against the Blackwater operatives alleged to be the "shooters" at Nisour Square [in Baghdad, Iraq]. Seventeen innocent Iraqis were killed in the shooting and more than 20 others wounded. In the brief, prosecutors asked that the indictment of the Blackwater men be reinstated. Then in April, five of Erik Prince's top deputies were hit with a fifteen-count indictment by a federal grand jury on conspiracy, weapons and obstruction of justice charges. Among those indicted were Prince's longtime number-two man, former Blackwater president Gary Jackson, former vice presidents William Matthews and Ana Bundy and Prince's former legal counsel Andrew Howell. Former Blackwater employees have made serious allegations in sworn declarations and in Grand Jury testimony about murder, gun smuggling, prostitution, destruction of evidence and a slew of other alleged crimes.

Clearly, none of this is cause for major concern at the White House.

Over the past two weeks, Blackwater has been awarded more than $200 million in new contracts by the Obama administration. One is a $120 million arrangement with the US State Department for security services in Afghanistan, the other, worth $100 million, is for protecting CIA operations and operatives in Afghanistan and other hot zones globally. Blackwater has spent heavily this year on lobbyists—particularly Democratic ones. In the first quarter of 2010, the company spent more than $500,000 for the services of Stuart Eizenstat, a well-connected Democratic lobbyist who served in the (President Bill) Clinton and (President Jimmy) Carter administrations. Eizenstat heads the international practice for the powerhouse law and lobbying firm Covington and Burling.

"Blackwater has undergone some serious changes," an unnamed U.S. official told *The Washington Post*. "They've had to prove to the government that they're a responsible outfit. Having satisfied every legal requirement, they have the right to compete for contracts. They have people who do good work, at times in some very dangerous places. Nobody should forget that, either."

What does Blackwater have to do to be determined an illegitimate player?

Let's also not forget that like McChrystal, Erik Prince was recently featured in an entertainment magazine. In January, *Vanity Fair* profiled Prince. In the article Prince and his associates didn't speak disparagingly about the commander in chief or the vice president, but Prince did appear to reveal details of classified US operations and the existence of a covert CIA assassination team, trained and organized by Prince, that planned hits in various countries, including inside Germany, a key US ally.

Maybe if some reporter catches Erik Prince and his cronies engaged in drunken, profanity-laced diatribes aimed at the White House and Commander in Chief, something would really change. If they used the phrase "bite me" when speaking of the vice president or embarrassed poor little Richard Holbrooke or called the National Security Advisor a "clown," maybe the administration would decide it was inappropriate to continue Blackwater's "services."

There's no doubt, under the Uniform Code of Military Conduct, McChrystal was rightly relieved of his duties. But in the end, it was McChrystal's words—not his actions—that sunk his ship. Blackwater's ship of misconduct, crime and murder will apparently sail on for the foreseeable future, at least until their words, instead of their bullets, strike the wrong people.

UPDATE: I [Jeremy Scahill] just interviewed Rep. Jan Schakowsky, the leading lawmaker opposing Blackwater. A member of the House Intelligence Committee, Schakowsky cannot confirm details of Blackwater's work for the CIA, but regarding the report they had been hired again by the CIA, she said: "It's just outrageous. What does Blackwater have to do to be determined an illegitimate player? While some of Blackwater's personnel do good work, its employees have proven to be untrustworthy with weapons in combat zones. Whether they are at the center of a mission or are doing static security, we should not be using Blackwater employees. The CIA should not be doing business with this company no matter how many name changes it undergoes." Schakowsky added: "If the reason for using Blackwater is that the government lacks capacity or can't find any reputable firm with this capacity, then that's a serious problem that needs to be confronted head on."

14

Corruption Pervades American Life

Mortimer B. Zuckerman

Mortimer B. Zuckerman is chairman and editor in chief of U.S. News & World Report *and chairman and co-publisher of the* New York Daily News. *He is a frequent commentator on world affairs and regularly appears on* MSNBC *and* The McLaughlin Group.

Americans of every age and circumstance seem to be involved in some form of cheating. While the banking industry and financiers such as Bernie Madoff provoke outrage for their greed and utter lack of conscience, other Americans from well-known athletes to average students are also engaged in cheating. US President Barack Obama urged Americans to change this destructive behavior in his 2009 inaugural address, calling for a "new era of responsibility." Americans would do well to heed his words and move the nation away from an environment of corruption.

Is this a nation of cheaters? We seem to be awash with them. Corporate executives cheat; athletes cheat; students cheat, beginning in middle school and extending into high school and college; and even teachers cheat. Are the seeds of adult corruption—for that's what it is—sown in the early years of schooling? Beginning in the '80s, there seems to have been a marriage of the me generation with [the character] Gordon Gekko's notion in the movie *Wall Street* that "greed is good." Did our admiration of wealth lead us to overlook, even forgive, the means of its attainment?

Beating the System Is an Attractive Notion

Many people seem to like beating the system, particularly if they see it as rigged or unfair. Nearly everyone feels that he or she pays too much in taxes and that others don't pay enough. The result is cheating on taxes to the tune of hundreds of billions of dollars a year. Similarly, people watch illegal DVDs because they feel legitimate prices are "a rip-off," they fudge insurance claims because insurance rates "are sky high," or they pocket office supplies because "the company can afford it."

The climax of this epidemic of cheating can be seen in those multimillions of bonus dollars accepted by bankers and investment stewards who were deified while presiding over institutions they were busy breaking. Take the Bernie Madoff case, in which he reportedly confessed to relieving his investors of $50 billion through a Ponzi scheme that would have made Charles Ponzi jealous. One thinks back to the difference a hundred years ago when the legendary banker J.P. Morgan testified before Congress in 1912. Dismissing the notion that commercial credit was based on money or property, he said, "No, sir. The first thing is character.... A man I do not trust could not get money from me on all the bonds in Christendom."

Many people seem to like beating the system, particularly if they see it as rigged or unfair.

The supposed masters of the universe seemed to have lost a moral compass and the power of reason, borrowing unconscionable amounts in relation to their equity, circulating financial documents they didn't seem to understand. They have proved to be greedy pretenders who created a disaster and, in the process, ruined vast numbers of people.

In his brilliant inaugural address, President [Barack] Obama said, "What is required of us now is a new era of responsibility." Clearly, his administration will impose regulations to cover the shadow banking system that abandoned responsibility. But the president also called for us to "set aside childish things." Nothing is more childish than the conduct of athletic heroes like Barry Bonds using performance-enhancing drugs to break Hank Aaron's home run record; Roger Clemens using anabolic steroids to extend his career; and New England Patriots' coach Bill Belichick apparently having the practices of an opponent secretly filmed. Once upon a time, athletes were role models!

Cheating Is Pervasive Among Students

A sickness lies in our educational system. A nationwide survey of 36,000 secondary students reported in the Educational Forum found that 60 percent admitted cheating on tests and assignments. Furthermore, 80 percent of the 3,000 students chosen for scholastic recognition in the prestigious *Who's Who Among American High School Students* acknowledged cheating on teacher-made and state tests. In a Rutgers University sample of 24,000 high school students, 64 percent admitted to one or more instance of "serious" cheating on exams, and a whopping 95 percent confessed to some form of cheating in their high school careers. According to the Josephson Institute Center for Youth Ethics, 40 percent thought you could not succeed in the United States without lying, cheating, or stealing; roughly one third of boys and one fourth of girls admitted stealing from a store within the past year; and roughly 64 percent cheated on a test, while 38 percent did so two or more times. More than 1 in 4 confessed that they lied on at least one question on the survey itself. Yet, ironically, they have a high self-image: 93 percent said they were satisfied with their personal ethics and character. A group of cheats who think they're angels!

Technology has made cheating easy. Students can E-mail homework to a network of classmates or text-message each other during exams. More than half of U.S. college students own up to some kind of cheating, not just copying other students' answers and crib sheets but using things like the term-paper mills on the Internet that proudly offer hundreds of thousands of essays that will meet virtually any college requirement.

Even prospective teachers being tested in order to qualify to teach in one state's public schools had to be thumb-printed because people had sent ringers to take examinations for them. This from those who are supposed to create classrooms where learning takes on more importance than having the right answer.

We must find a way to explain to kids how necessary it is to do the right thing and avoid what the late Sen. Daniel Patrick Moynihan called "defining deviancy down"—that is, lowering the bar on bad behavior to make it acceptable. Young people admire President Obama. Let them heed what he said in such a timely manner.

Organizations to Contact

The editors have compiled the following list of organizations concerned with the issues debated in this book. The descriptions are derived from materials provided by the organizations. All have publications or information available for interested readers. The list was compiled on the date of publication of the present volume; names; addresses, phone and fax numbers, and e-mail and Internet addresses may change. Be aware that many organizations take several weeks or longer to respond to inquiries, so allow as much time as possible.

AFL-CIO
815 Sixteenth Street NW, Washington, DC   20006
fax: (202) 637-5012
website: www.aflcio.org

The AFL-CIO is a federation of labor unions whose stated goal is to bring economic and social justice to workplaces and communities. The AFL-CIO website includes Executive Paywatch, which monitors the salaries and retirement packages of CEOs in relationship to the American workforce.

American Accounting Association
5717 Bessie Drive, Sarasota, FL   34233-2399
(941) 921-7747
e-mail: info@aaahq.org
website: http://aaahq.org/

The American Accounting Association is a professional organization that aims to promote excellence in accounting education, research, and practice.

The Business Roundtable
1717 Rhode Island Avenue NW, Suite 800
Washington, DC   20036

(202) 872-1260

website: www.businessroundtable.org

The Business Roundtable is an association of chief executive officers of leading US companies. It conducts research, publishes position papers, and advocates public policies that support economic growth, a dynamic global economy, and a productive US workforce.

The Center for a Just Society

1220 L Street NW, Suite 100-371, Washington, DC 20005

e-mail: infor@centerforajustsociety.org

website: www.centerforajustsociety.org

The Center for a Just Society promotes principles of human dignity and social justice in law, public policy, and civil debate. The Center believes that in a pluralistic society, religious values can still provide guidance in the shaping of public policy so that individuals, businesses, and public institutions are held accountable for their actions.

CorpWatch

2958 24th Street, San Francisco, CA 94110

(415) 641-1633

website: http://corpwatch.org

CorpWatch is a global watchdog organization that investigates corporate fraud and corruption. It engages in independent media activism and advocates for democratic control over corporations.

The Council of Better Business Bureaus (CBBB)

4200 Wilson Blvd. Suite 800, Arlington, VA 22203

(703) 276-0100

website: www.bbb.org

The membership of the Council of Better Business Bureaus (CBBB) includes three hundred national corporations and more than three hundred thousand businesses nationwide.

CBBB promotes ethical relationships between businesses and the public through voluntary self-regulation, consumer, and business education.

CSRwire

250 Albany Street, Springfield, MA 01105
(802) 251-0110
e-mail: help@csrwire.com
website: www.csrwire.com

CSRwire is a global source of corporate social responsibility (CSR) and sustainability news. Founded in 1999 to advance the movement towards a more economically-just and environmentally-sustainable society and away from single bottom line capitalism, CSRwire encourages new standards of corporate citizenship.

Ethics Resource Center

2345 Crystal Drive, Suite 201, Arlington, VA 22202
(703) 647-2185
e-mail: ethics@ethics.org
website: www.ethics.org

The Ethics Resource Center is a non-profit organization that advances understanding of practices that promote ethical conduct. It conducts research, publishes white papers and educational resources, and sponsors a Fellows Program for corporate ethics officers and academics interested in organizational ethics.

Government Accountability Project

1612 K Street NW, Suite 1100, Washington, DC 20006
(202) 457-0034
e-mail: info@whistleblowers.org
website: www.whistleblower.org

The Government Accountability Project is a non-profit interest group that promotes government and corporate accountability by advancing occupational free speech, defending whistleblowers, and empowering citizen activists.

National Association of Corporate Directors

1133 Twenty-first Street NW, Suite 700
Washington, DC 20036
(202) 775-0509
website: www.nacdonline.org

The National Association of Corporate Directors focuses on the corporate governance needs of directors and boards. It offers educational programs and conducts independent research to identify best practices for greater board effectiveness.

Organisation for Economic Co-operation and Development (OECD)

OECD Washington Center, Washington, DC 20036-4922
(202) 785-6323 • fax: (202) 785-0350
e-mail: washington.contact@oecd.org
website: www.oecdwash.org

The mission of the Organisation for Economic Co-operation and Development (OECD) is to promote policies that will improve the economic and social well-being of people around the world. The OECD provides a forum in which governments can work together to share experiences and seek solutions to common problems. It works with governments to understand what drives economic, social, and environmental change.

Securities and Exchange Commission (SEC)

100 F Street NE, Washington, DC 20549
(202) 942-8088
website: http://sec.gov

The Securities and Exchange Commission (SEC) is the US government agency that oversees securities markets to protect investors and facilitate capital formation. The SEC requires public companies to disclose certain kinds of financial and operational information to the public. This provides a common pool of knowledge that investors can use to judge for themselves whether to buy, sell or hold a particular security. Through the steady flow of timely, comprehensive, and accurate information the SEC can help people make sound investment decisions.

The United Nations Global Compact

The United Nations, New York, NY   10017
e-mail: globalcompact@un.org
website: http://un.globalcompact.org

The U.N. Global Compact is a voluntary initiative that relies on public accountability, transparency, and the enlightened self-interest of companies, labor, and civil society. It promotes responsible corporate citizenship, actively seeking solutions to contemporary problems related to globalization, sustainable development, and corporate responsibility in a multi-stakeholder context.

Weinberg Center for Corporate Governance

303 Alfred Lerner Hall, Newark, DE   19716
(302) 831-6157
website: www.lerner.udel.edu/centers/ccg

The University of Delaware's Weinberg Center for Corporate Governance seeks to propose progressive changes in corporate structure and management through education and interaction. The Center provides a forum for business leaders, members of corporate boards, the legal community, academics, practitioners, graduate and undergraduate students, and others interested in corporate governance issues to meet, interact, learn, and teach.

Bibliography

Book

Lucian Bebchuk and Jesse Fried — *Pay Without Performance: The Unfulfilled Promise of Executive Compensation.* Boston, MA: Harvard University Press, 2006.

Robert L. Bradley — *Capitalism at Work: Business, Government and Energy.* Salem, MA: M & M Scrivener Press, 2008.

David Callahan — *The Cheating Culture: Why More Americans Are Doing Wrong to Get Ahead.* Orlando, FL: Harcourt Books, 2004.

David Callahan — *Fortunes of Change: The Rise of the Liberal Rich and the Remaking of America.* Hoboken, NJ: John Wiley and Sons, 2010.

James Galbraith — *The Predator State: How Conservatives Abandoned the Free Market and Why Liberals Should Too.* New York: Free Press, 2008.

Gail Ghigna Hallas — *No Other Medicine: Inside View of Corporate Healthcare Corruption in Hospitals.* Charleston, SC: CreateSpace, 2011.

Umair Haque   *The New Capitalist Manifesto: Building a Disruptively Better Business.* Boston, MA: Harvard University Press, 2011.

Michael W. Hudson   *The Monster: How a Gang of Predatory Lenders and Wall Street Bankers Fleeced America—and Spawned a Global Crisis.* New York: Times Books, 2010.

David C. Korten   *Agenda for a New Economy: From Phantom Wealth to Real Wealth.* San Francisco, CA: Berret-Koehler Publishers, 2009.

T. Christian Miller   *Blood Money: Wasted Billions, Lost Lives, and Corporate Greed in Iraq.* Boston, MA: Little, Brown and Company, 2007.

Robert B. Reich   *Supercapitalism: The Transformation of Business, Democracy, and Everyday Life.* New York: Vintage Books, 2007.

Robert Scheer   *The Great American Stickup: How Reagan Republicans and Clinton Democrats Enriched Wall Street While Mugging Main Street.* New York: Nation Books, 2010.

Roy C. Smith   *Paper Fortunes: Modern Wall Street, Where It's Been and Where It's Going.* New York: St. Martin's Press, 2009.

Yves Smith — *ECONned: How Unenlightened Self Interest Undermined Democracy and Corrupted Capitalism.* New York: Palgrave MacMillan, 2010.

Joseph E. Stiglitz — *Freefall: America, Free Markets, and the Sinking of the World Economy.* New York: W. W. Norton & Company, 2010.

Matt Taibbi — *Griftopia: Bubble Machines, Vampire Squids, and the Long Con That is Breaking America.* New York: Spiegel and Grau, 2010.

Periodicals

Eleanor Bloxham — "Boards Take Heat for Political Spending," *CNN Money*, October 18, 2010.

David Callahan — "Why Aren't Big Pharma Execs Ever Punished?" HuffingtonPost.com, December 9, 2010.

Michelle Conlin — "Caught by Mistake in Foreclosure Web," *Charlotte Observer*, December 9, 2010.

The Economist — "Not for Sale," *The Economist*, January 20, 2010.

Peter Elkind and David Whitford — "The Untold Story of the BP Gulf Oil Disaster," *Fortune*, February 7, 2011.

Richard Eskow   "Afghanistan's 'Too Big to Fail' Bank
                     Is Failing—Guess Our System
                     Doesn't Work There Either,"
                     HuffingtonPost.com, February 2,
                     2011.

Daniel Fromson   "The Pause that Represses?
                     Coca-Cola's Controversies," *The
                     Atlantic*, October 18, 2010.

Alex Kingsbury   "Amid Recession, FBI Makes New
                     Push on Financial Crimes," *U.S. News
                     and World Report*, April 1, 2009.

Paul Krugman   "The Old Enemies," *New York Times*,
                     May 23, 2010.

Chisun Lee   "Higher Corporate Spending on
                     Election Ads Could Be All But
                     Invisible," ProPublica.com, March 10,
                     2010.

Anna Lenzer   "Typhoid, Tyranny and Tax Havens:
                     The Truth Behind America's
                     Trendiest Drink," *The Independent*,
                     November 8, 2009.

Robert Mazur   "Follow the Dirty Money," *New York
                     Times*, September 12, 2010.

Ole Ole Olson   "The Face of Corruption: Corporate
                     Campaign Contributions in the
                     Comcast/NBC Merger," *News Junkie
                     Post*, January 17, 2011.

Doug Pibel   "Get Free from Wall Street: An
                     Interview with David Korten," *Yes!
                     Magazine*, October 1, 2010.

Sam Pizzigati	"A Business Case for Greater Equality," *Too Much*, February 8, 2011.
Michael E. Porter and Mark R. Kramer	"The Big Idea: Creating Shared Value," *Harvard Business Review*, January/February 2011.
Robert Reich	"Corporate Rotten Eggs," Robertreich.org, August 20, 2010.
Robert Reich	"Why America's Two Economies Continue to Drift Apart, and What Washington Isn't Doing About It," Robertreich.org, December 14, 2010.
Mike Simpson	"The Good Corporate Citizen," *Leadership*, February 3, 2011.
Dean Starkman	"How Could 9000 Business Reporters Blow It?" *Mother Jones*, January/February 2009.
Joseph E. Stiglitz	"Justice for Some," *Project Syndicate*, November 4, 2010.
Jacob Sullum	"Where Is All This Corporate Corruption I Keep Hearing About?" *Reason*, September 3, 2009.
Matt Taibbi	"The Great American Bubble Machine," *Rolling Stone*, April 5, 2010.
Matt Taibbi	"Wall Street's Big Win," *Rolling Stone*, August 4, 2010.

| Nick Timaraos, Jessica Silver-Greenberg, Dan Fitzpatrick | "Mortgage Damage Spreads," *The Wall Street Journal*, October 16, 2010. |

Index

[8]